Antonia Clare

JJ Wilson

# speakout

Intermediate

Workbook with key

# CONTENTS

# CONTENTS

## VOCABULARY family

**1A** Rearrange the letters in italics to complete the sentences.

1 We see our *flexed dynamite* every week. <u>extended family</u>

2 My *transparent dagger* left India in 1920. _____

3 I researched my *fair oily myths* online. _____

4 Vincent is *a tree told* a famous actor. _____

5 It's always nice when *evil tears* come to stay. _____

6 I wish I knew more about my *cat sensor*. _____

7 When Ella's parents died, she *tied her in* an old house. _____

8 He doesn't know anyone on his mother's *emailed fifth soy*. _____

9 I asked Grandma about my French *torso*. _____

10 My son *fake treats* me; we have the same nose. _____

**B** Underline the correct alternatives.

I am probably more multicultural than most people. I have African, Polish and British ¹*inherits / roots / side*, and I was born in Germany. My ²*relative / inherited / extended* family is all over the world, with several of them in New Zealand and Australia. I know quite a lot about my ³*family story / family history / relative history* because my parents told me about it when I was a child. My ⁴*great / greater / grand* grandparents on my father's ⁵*sides / end / side* of the family were from Poland, while my mother's ⁶*relatives / sides / related* are from Nigeria. I don't know much about my ⁷*take after / family extended / ancestors* before the 1900s, except that I am ⁸*relative / related to / inherited* the chief of a tribe in Nigeria.

## GRAMMAR question forms

**2A** Circle the question with the correct form.

1 a) What you keeps awake at night?
   b) What keeps you awake at night? *(circled)*

2 a) Who you wanted to be when you were a child?
   b) Who did you want to be when you were a child?

3 a) Who taught you a valuable lesson, and what was it?
   b) Who did teach you a valuable lesson, and what was it?

4 a) You ever wish you lived in a different time?
   b) Do you ever wish you lived in a different time?

5 a) What type of music you do listen to?
   b) What type of music do you listen to?

6 a) As a child, did you like school?
   b) As a child, did you to like school?

7 a) When did you first think of yourself as an adult?
   b) When you first thought of yourself as an adult?

8 a) What one thing do you always worry?
   b) What one thing do you always worry about?

**B** Match questions 1–8 in Exercise 2A with answers a)–h).

a) Tom Cruise or Johnny Depp.   2

b) Yes. I loved every minute of it!

c) My weight. I'm permanently on a diet.

d) The sound of my husband snoring.

e) When I bought my first car.

f) No. I like the twenty-first century just fine.

g) My brother taught me to stand up for myself.

h) All types: jazz, rap, classical, rock.

**3** Circle the correct options to complete the text.

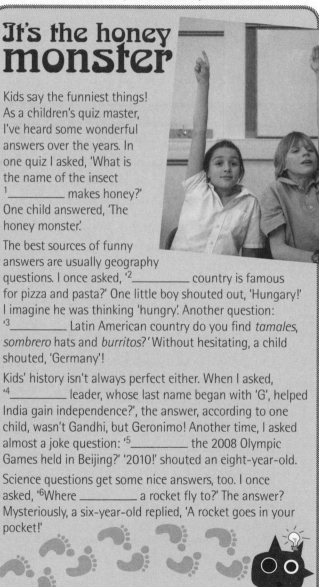

# It's the honey monster

Kids say the funniest things! As a children's quiz master, I've heard some wonderful answers over the years. In one quiz I asked, 'What is the name of the insect ¹_____ makes honey?' One child answered, 'The honey monster.'

The best sources of funny answers are usually geography questions. I once asked, '²_____ country is famous for pizza and pasta?' One little boy shouted out, 'Hungary!' I imagine he was thinking 'hungry'. Another question: '³_____ Latin American country do you find *tamales*, *sombrero* hats and *burritos*?' Without hesitating, a child shouted, 'Germany'!

Kids' history isn't always perfect either. When I asked, '⁴_____ leader, whose last name began with 'G', helped India gain independence?', the answer, according to one child, wasn't Gandhi, but Geronimo! Another time, I asked almost a joke question: '⁵_____ the 2008 Olympic Games held in Beijing?' '2010!' shouted an eight-year-old.

Science questions get some nice answers, too. I once asked, '⁶Where _____ a rocket fly to?' The answer? Mysteriously, a six-year-old replied, 'A rocket goes in your pocket!'

1 a) who      b) what      c) which

2 a) Which    b) Whose     c) Where

3 a) In which  b) What      c) At which

4 a) Who      b) Which is   c) Which

5 a) When did  b) When were  c) What year

6 a) is       b) do        c) does

**4A** ▶ 1.1 Listen and write the questions you hear.

1 _____

2 _____

3 _____

4 _____

5 _____

6 _____

**B** Listen again and repeat, paying attention to the intonation.

## LISTENING

**5A** ▶ 1.2 Listen to three people answering the questions below. Write their answers.

Which family member influenced you the most? How?

| | **Who?** | **How?** |
|---|---|---|
| Clyde | _____ | _____ |
| Luciana | _____ | _____ |
| Austin | _____ | _____ |

**B** Listen again and answer the questions.

1 What expression did Clyde's mother always use?

_____

2 Where did Clyde travel to when he was young?

_____

3 How long did Luciana live with her grandparents?

_____

4 What was her grandfather's 'major thing'?

_____

5 What story did Austin's Uncle Charlie tell?

_____

6 What did Austin's mother say about Uncle Charlie?

_____

**C** Read the extracts from the recording. What do you think the words and phrases in bold mean? Match them with meanings a)–f).

1 So **in that respect** I think my mother really influenced me.

2 He was very **tough**.

3 He could be very **gentle**.

4 He always **saw the bright side of life**.

5 He was built like a tank. I mean **massive**.

6 He fought a crocodile **with his bare hands**.

a) strong and determined

b) extremely big

c) without using a weapon or tool

d) in this way

e) was optimistic

f) kind and careful not to hurt anyone

## WRITING emails of introduction: formal and informal

**6A** Read the purposes of two emails. Which email needs to be formal?

1 Introduce myself to a member of my host family in Spain before I visit.

2 Introduce myself as the new chairperson of the Teachers' Association.

**B** Read the emails and underline the correct alternatives.

> To: psanchez@yoohoo.es
> Subject: hi!
> From: danielagjones@hitmail.com
>
> [1]*Hi Pilar / Dear Madam Pilar,*
>
> [2]*I am writing to greet you. / How are you?* As you know, I'm going to stay with you this summer. I [3]*have decided to / thought I'd* send an email to introduce myself. My name's Daniela, but my friends call me Danny, and I hope you will, too.
>
> I'm eighteen years old and at university here in Manchester, studying Business and Economics. I've got lots of hobbies. I love horse riding, swimming, listening to music, and I also play the flute. My favourite hobby, though, is dancing. I [4]*am particularly keen on / really like* samba and salsa.
>
> I [5]*can't wait to stay / look forward to staying* with you in Spain, though my Spanish isn't very good! [6]*Hope / I do hope* to hear from you soon.
>
> Danny

> To: membership@taas.com
> Subject: Introductions
> From: hatquistj@ltsu.edu
>
> [7]*Dear members / Hello everybody,*
>
> [8]*I'm writing to say hi / I am writing to introduce myself.* As many of you know, I will begin in the role of chairperson of the Teachers' Association of Amlen State at the end of this month. [9]*I would like to take this opportunity / I really want* to outline my major plans for the Association over the coming year.
>
> I am a maths and physics teacher. I have been in the profession for over forty years in a variety of roles: teacher, administrative assistant, head teacher, and school inspector.
>
> My first priority is to increase membership. In the last six years we have seen a decrease of almost 30% in our numbers. I have various proposals for achieving this, which [10]*I'll tell you about / I will explain* during our first meeting next month.
>
> [11]*I look forward to working with you all / See you all soon.*
>
> [12]*All the best / Yours sincerely,*
>
> Jacqueline Hatquist

**C** Read the instructions and write an email (120–150 words).

You are going on an adventure trip for students of English. You will join ten other students from all over the world on a one-month tour of India. The tour will include cultural visits and two hours of English lessons every day. Write an email of introduction to the other students.

## GRAMMAR review of verb tenses

**1** Complete the conversations with the correct form of the verbs in brackets.

1 A: I need a holiday, but flights _____ (be) always expensive at this time of year.

  B: That's true, but I _____ (find) a cheap flight to Mexico on the net yesterday.

2 A: Grace _____ (win) the lottery last week!

  B: That's right. She _____ (sleep) when her brother called to tell her.

3 A: I _____ (not like) football.

  B: Why _____ you _____ (not tell) me earlier? The tickets cost £70 each!

4 A: _____ you _____ (hear) about the accident last week?

  B: Yes, the boys _____ (drive) along Court Street when a motorbike hit the car.

5 A: _____ you _____ (need) somewhere to stay? I have a spare room.

  B: No, it's OK. I _____ (stay) with my sister.

6 A: I _____ (read) a novel called *The Road* at the moment.

  B: Oh yes. I found it so boring that I _____ (not finish) it.

7 A: I like an early start, so I _____ (get up) at six every morning.

  B: Me too. I always _____ (leave) the house by seven.

8 A: John! Are you ready? We _____ (wait) for you!

  B: OK, here I am! Sorry about that. I _____ (look) for my hat! I couldn't find it anywhere.

**2** Match beginnings a) and b) with endings i) and ii).

1 a) Do you use the computer?  *ii*

  b) Are you using the computer?  *i*

  i) I need it for a few minutes.

  ii) Or is everything done by phone?

2 a) She tries to work

  b) She's trying to work

  i) , so please be quiet.

  ii) on her book for two hours every day.

3 a) It doesn't snow

  b) It isn't snowing,

  i) much in New Mexico.

  ii) so we can go out now.

4 a) What are you doing

  b) What do you do

  i) for a living?

  ii) now? Do you want to go for a coffee?

5 a) He was playing squash

  b) He played squash

  i) for the team last year.

  ii) when he broke his ankle.

## VOCABULARY relationships

**3A** Put the words in the box into categories 1–4.

employee  fiancée  fiancé  classmate  pupil  boss
team-mate  godfather  godmother  member

1 Person you work with:
_____

2 Person who studies:
_____

3 Person you are close to (almost family):
_____

4 Person you do a hobby with:
_____

**B** Complete the sentences with the words in Exercise 3A.

1 This is Marianna, my _____. We're getting married next year.

2 Dave is my _____. We're both in Year 12 at Cokethorpe High School.

3 She asked her _____ for some time off work, but he said no.

4 I'm a _____ of a swimming club. We meet twice a week at the sports centre.

5 Luisa got 100% in her exam. She's the best _____ in my class.

6 He's an _____ of GEO Foods. He's been there for six years.

7 When I was born, my father asked John, his best friend, to be my _____.

8 Leticia is my _____. We play in the same basketball team.

**4A** Underline the stressed syllable in the words in italics.

1 He was an *employee* here.

2 I had a wonderful *mentor*.

3 All *pupils* wear a uniform.

4 We were *team-mates* for years.

5 Have you met my *fiancée*?

6 Talk to your *partner*.

7 She's my *godmother*.

8 That club is for *members* only.

**B** ▶ 1.3 Listen and check. Then listen and shadow the sentences (say them at the same time).

## chatzone1com

### Men and Women – What They Say About Each Other

1. The battle of the sexes has probably been going on since the first caveman left his dirty dishes on the floor of the cave. A subject of endless discussion, it has inspired a million jokes and articles and almost as many books.

2. However, a recent study tells us that men and women really do think differently. Our brains are built in a different way. The results of the study suggest that men have better spatial perception (driving, ball sports), while women's brains equip them better for remembering words and speaking fluently.

3. The scientists examined only a small part of the brain, and they say that further research needs to be done. Here at *chatzone1* we have done some less scientific research. We asked people, 'What are the differences between the sexes?' Here are their answers.

### What women say about men

4. Men remember useless information, like how fast an aeroplane can go, even if they'll never fly one. (Heather)

If you ask a man a question, he'll always have an answer, even if it's the wrong one. (Aisha)

Men do things first, and think about the risks later. (Candy)

Men cannot watch sport on TV and talk to women at the same time. (Mai)

### What men say about men

5. Men know that common house spiders aren't as dangerous as rattlesnakes. (Daniel)

Men can drive without looking at themselves in the mirror every ten seconds. (Ron)

Men can watch a whole film without interrupting to ask, 'Who is he?' 'What's her job?' 'Does he like her?' (Alfred)

When men want something, they ask for it instead of making a comment distantly related to the subject and hoping their partner will guess what the real subject is. (Guy)

### What men say about women

6. Women couldn't invent weapons that kill, only weapons that make you feel really guilty until you say sorry. (Kent)

While men speak in sentences, women speak in paragraphs. (Sergio)

Women are happy to own twenty CDs, while men need 200. (Steve)

Women order salad, then eat the man's chips. (Kazeem)

### What women say about women

7. Women have natural instincts about what is dangerous for babies. (Linda)

Women notice when something is dirty or needs replacing. (Carol)

Only women can understand other women. (Xun)

Women have a calendar in their brains: we remember birthdays and anniversaries easily. (Avril)

---

## READING

**5A** Do you think statements 1–4 are about men or women? Who said them: men or women?

1 They do things first, and think about the risks later.

2 They remember useless information.

3 They notice when something is dirty or needs replacing.

4 They always remember birthdays and anniversaries.

**B** Read the text and check.

**C** Write the name of the person who makes similar statements to the ones below.

1 Men hate to say, 'I don't know'. *Aisha*

2 Men cannot 'multi-task'; they can only concentrate on one thing at a time. _____

3 Men are very direct when they need something. _____

4 Women are more fluent than men when they speak. _____

5 Women are more maternal; they understand what is good for young children. _____

6 Women have better memories for dates than men. _____

**D** Find words in the text to match definitions 1–5.

1 the ability to see the position, size or shape of things (paragraph 2) _____

2 give you the tools or abilities that you need (paragraph 2) _____

3 more or to a greater degree (paragraph 3) _____

4 not closely (paragraph 5) _____

5 natural abilities or feelings that make people and animals know something (paragraph 7) _____

## VOCABULARY PLUS collocations with *take/get/do/go*

**6** Complete the phrases with *take*, *get*, *do* or *go*. Use each verb three times.

| | | | |
|---|---|---|---|
| 1 | *get* a job | 7 | _____ grey |
| 2 | _____ off coffee | 8 | _____ her a favour |
| 3 | _____ part in a quiz | 9 | _____ responsibility |
| 4 | _____ some research | 10 | _____ angry |
| 5 | _____ my homework | 11 | _____ up the guitar |
| 6 | _____ on with people | 12 | _____ for a walk |

## VOCABULARY interview advice

**1** Match 1–8 with a)–h) to make advice.

1 Don't avoid eye
2 The most important thing is to be
3 Make sure you show
4 You must arrive on
5 Shake hands
6 Make sure you dress
7 Don't always answer
8 Before the interview, do

a) some research about the company.
b) briefly. Try to give a full response.
c) smartly. Maybe wear a suit.
d) contact. Look at them during the interview.
e) enthusiasm. Smile and ask questions.
f) firmly with your interviewers.
g) prepared. Think about what they will ask you.
h) time. Don't be late!

## FUNCTION talking about yourself

**2A** Add the vowels to complete the conversations.

**Conversation 1**
A: C__ __ld I __sk a q__ __st__ __n?
B: Sure. Go ahead.
A: Will this type of project become common?
B: In my __p__n__ __n, architecture will become more environmentally friendly.

**Conversation 2**
A: Th__r__ __r__ a c__ __pl__ __ __ th__ngs I'd l__k__ t__ __sk __b__ __ __.
B: OK.
A: How do you see your future in our company?
B: F__r me, th__ m__st __mp__rt__nt th__ng is to keep developing and learning the job.

**Conversation 3**
A: I h__v__ a q__ __ry.
B: Yes? Go ahead.
A: A lot of people criticised you because of the cuts in funding for education. Did you ever think about resigning from the government?
B: One th__ng I'd l__k__ t__ s__y is th__t compared to other governments, we invested a lot of money in education.

**Conversation 4**
A: Earlier, you mentioned your latest film. C__n I __sk you __b__ __t th__t?
B: Yes, of course.
A: Was it difficult not being the star?
B: I'd h__v__ t__ s__y 'yes'. In my last four films I always had the biggest part.

**B** Match pictures A–D with conversations 1–4 in Exercise 2A.

## LEARN TO use two-word responses

**3** Circle the correct option to complete the conversations.

1 A: Is it OK if I check my emails?
  B: _____. That's fine.
    a) Go ahead   b) That's right   c) I understand

2 A: Are you interested in free medical insurance?
  B: _____. How do I sign up?
    a) You're correct   b) Yes, definitely   c) No problem

3 A: My dog is ill, so I can't come to work today.
  B: _____. Will you be in tomorrow?
    a) You're correct   b) Please continue   c) I see

4 A: Hi, Nazir. I'm going to be about fifteen minutes late.
  B: _____. There's no hurry.
    a) Yes, definitely   b) That's right   c) No problem

5 A: I can't travel in June – my wife's expecting a baby.
  B: _____. We'll make sure there's no travel until at least August.
    a) I understand   b) Go ahead   c) You're welcome

6 A: Do you live at 106 West Smith Road?
  B: Yes. _____.
    a) That's right   b) No problem   c) You're welcome

7 A: So the answer is probably 15,997.
  B: _____. But how did you reach the answer?
    a) You're correct   b) No problem   c) Go ahead

8 A: Thank you so much for letting me use your motorbike.
  B: _____. Did you have fun?
    a) Yes, definitely   b) I see   c) You're welcome

9 A: Excuse the interruption. I'm just showing Mr Liu the classrooms. _____.
  B: Oh, OK. So, students, turn to page 33.
    a) I see   b) You're welcome   c) Please continue

10 A: Are you able to work next weekend?
  B: _____. We need to finish the project, don't we?
    a) Go ahead   b) Of course   c) I understand

## VOCABULARY types of story

### 1A Complete the words to describe types of story.

1 *Terminator* is one of the best ever __ct__ __n films.
2 *Walk the Line* is a b__ __p__c of the musician Johnny Cash.
3 *Avatar* won an award for best f__nt__sy film.
4 I enjoy all film genres, particularly historical or p__r__ __d dr__m__.
5 *New in Town* is a r__m__nt__c c__m__dy about an ambitious woman from Miami who moves to a small town In Minnesota, in America's mid-west.
6 *The Wizard of Oz* is a classic children's __dv__nt__r__ story.
7 *2012*, one of the biggest Hollywood d__s__st__r films ever made, shows the end of the world as we know it. The special effects are truly spectacular.
8 Cr__m__ films range from Hitchcock's thr__ll__r *Vertigo* to the dark c__m__dy *Pulp Fiction*.
9 *He Who Must Live* is a d__c__dr__m__ about the life of Fidel Castro.

### B Which words in Exercise 1A could be used to describe these films?

1 *Nowhere Boy* talks about John Lennon while he was at school and art college in 1950s Liverpool.
2 *Supervolcano* is based on what would happen if the volcano in Yellowstone National Park erupted.
3 In *My Best Friend's Wedding*, best friends Julianne Potter and Michael O'Neil promise to marry each other if they are still single at the age of twenty-eight.
4 *Daybreakers*: It is the year 2019, and a plague has transformed much of the world's population into vampires.
5 *Die Hard* stars Bruce Willis as a policeman battling against terrorists.
6 *Murder on the Orient Express*: When his train is stopped by deep snow, detective Hercule Poirot is called on to solve a murder when the body of one of the passengers is discovered.

## GRAMMAR present perfect/past simple

### 2 Underline the correct alternatives.

1 A: I *'ve never been / didn't go* to Hollywood.
   B: Haven't you? I *went / 've been* there last year.
2 A: How many films *have you acted / did you act* in so far?
   B: I *'ve acted / acted* in seventeen films up to now.
3 A: He's only twenty-two years old, but he *travelled / has travelled* all around the world.
   B: Really? Which countries *did he visit / has he visited*?
4 A: She *has won / won* four Oscars for her performances.
   B: That's right. She *has won / won* an award for Best Actress last month.
5 A: They *have lived / lived* in California for twenty years.
   B: When *did they move / have they moved* to Texas?
6 A: *Have you been / Were you* here for a long time?
   B: Yes. I *arrived / have arrived* over an hour ago.
7 A: We *'ve been married / were married* for forty years now.
   B: Do you remember the first day we *'ve met / met*?
8 A: *Did you enjoy / Have you enjoyed* the film?
   B: I *didn't have / haven't had* time to watch it yet.

### 3 Rewrite the second sentence so that it means the same as the first. Use the correct form of the words in capitals.

1 I met Ella ten years ago.   KNOW
   I *'ve known* Ella for ten years.
2 She went to Mumbai four weeks ago.   BE
   She _____ in Mumbai for four weeks.
3 They started the business in 2009.   WORK
   They _____ together since 2009.
4 We moved into the house six months ago.   LIVE
   We _____ this house for six months.
5 The last time I saw Robbie was two weeks ago.   SEE
   I _____ for two weeks.
6 This is my third visit to London.   BE
   I _____ three times.

### 4A ▶ 2.1 Listen and complete the conversations.

1 A: Have you been here before?
   B: Yes, _____ Naples a few times.
2 A: Have you had time to see the museum yet?
   B: No, _____ time.
3 A: Did you find your hotel OK?
   B: Yes, _____ the hotel without any problems.
4 A: Have you got your guidebook?
   B: Oh no. I _____ it in my room.
5 A: Have you had any lunch?
   B: Yes, _____ eaten.
6 A: Have you enjoyed your stay?
   B: Yes, _____ a wonderful time.

### B Listen again and shadow the answers.

## VOCABULARY PLUS prepositions

**5** Underline the correct preposition to complete the sentences.

1 I'll see you *at / on / in* lunchtime.

2 We often cook outside *at / in / on* the summer.

3 I start work at 8.30a.m. *at / on / in* Monday.

4 I try not to go out alone *at / on / in* night.

5 I just heard it *at / on / in* the radio.

6 *At / On / In* the end, we decided to take a taxi.

7 I'm sorry. I took your coat *at / by / in* mistake.

8 Please be quick. We're *at / by / in* a hurry.

9 Wait there. I'll be with you *at / on / in* a moment.

10 We found the museum completely *at / by / in* chance.

11 I'm afraid Mr Reeves is away *at / on / in* business. Can I help?

12 Nobody wanted to come with me, so I went *at / on / in* my own.

## READING

**6A** What do you know about James Dean? Are the statements true (T) or false (F)?

1 James Dean became famous for his role in the film *Rebel Without a Cause*.

2 He died in a car accident when he was just twenty-one years old.

3 He was speeding in his car at the time of the accident.

4 When he was younger, he nearly died in a motorcycle accident.

5 His favourite drink was whisky.

**B** Read the article on the right and check your answers. Correct the false statements.

**C** Circle the correct option to answer the questions.

1 Why do people come to Hollywood?

a) Because it's dangerous.

b) To follow their dreams.

c) To meet other actors.

2 Why was James Dean nicknamed 'America's Rebel'?

a) He played a teenager in the film *Rebel Without a Cause*.

b) He was friends with another actor, Ronald Reagan.

c) Teenagers respected his rebellious attitude.

3 What did he do before he arrived in Hollywood?

a) He performed dangerous stunts on television.

b) He raced motorbikes.

c) He worked in a restaurant.

4 Why did Dean argue with his father?

a) His father caught him drinking whisky.

b) He crashed his father's car.

c) His father didn't want him to be an actor.

# FOREVER YOUNG: THE HOLLYWOOD HERO WHO DIED YOUNG

'Dream as if you'll live forever; live as if you'll die tomorrow.'

1 The dream is the same for everyone; actors, dancers, singers, filmmakers. They go to Hollywood looking for money, success, fame and power. And many come to Hollywood as young people, barely out of their teens. But Hollywood can be a dangerous place, and some of Hollywood's heroes even lose their lives because of it. But although they die young, they are heroes forever, immortalised in film history.

2 One such hero was James Dean. Dean once said 'Dream as if you'll live forever; live as if you'll die tomorrow'. Arriving in Hollywood as a young man, James Dean quickly became a star. In the film *Rebel Without a Cause*, Dean showed teenage angst at its best, and he captured the world with his casual style and rebellious attitude. It was an attitude that he held both on-screen and off, and teenagers everywhere found a hero they could both respect and admire. Soon, he was more popular than even his own screen idol, Marlon Brando, and he was nicknamed 'America's Rebel' by Ronald Reagan.

3 Always the rebel, Dean was afraid of nothing. Before becoming famous, he worked as a stuntman for a TV show. Dean loved his car, a silver Porsche 550 Spyder, and it was in this car that on September 30, 1955, Dean crashed and died from his injuries. He was just twenty-four years old. Even though his career in Hollywood was short, he only made three films, he made a lasting impression on everybody who watched him, and even on future generations. James Dean will be forever young.

4 There are many myths about James Dean, but only some of them are true. James Dean loved speed. When he was younger, he had a motorcycle accident and lost his two front teeth. People assumed that Dean was speeding at the time of his car crash – he had been stopped by police for speeding just two hours earlier. But experts now believe that Dean was travelling at 55 mph, and that the accident was just unlucky. As a young man, Dean was a rebel at home. He was thrown out of his father's house when they argued about Dean wanting an acting career, rather than a career in Law. And finally, on-screen James Dean is shown getting into a fight after drinking whisky, but off-screen his favourite drink was coffee.

**D** Find words or phrases in the text to match definitions 1–5.

1 still very young/in their early twenties (paragraph 1) _____

2 made famous for a long time (paragraph 1) _____

3 opinions or behaviour which are against authority (paragraph 2) _____

4 an opinion or feeling about someone/something that you have for a long time (paragraph 3) _____

5 thought something was true (paragraph 4) _____

## LISTENING

**1A  Read the introduction to a radio programme. Are the statements true (T) or false (F)?**

1  A 'flashbulb memory' is a memory of an important event.

2  You do not usually remember small details with a flashbulb memory.

### FLASHBULB MEMORIES
#### – WHERE WERE YOU THEN?

Do you remember where you were when an important event occurred? Can you remember who you were with? Then you may have what is called a 'flashbulb memory'. In 1977, two psychologists, Roger Brown and James Kulick, used the term 'flashbulb memories' to talk about people's recollections of the John F. Kennedy assassination. They suggested that, like a camera's flashbulb, when a truly shocking event happens, the brain 'takes a picture' of the moment when you learn about the event. This enables us to remember, sometimes in great detail, events of an emotional significance to us. Tune in to Radio 6 *Real Lives* and listen to some of the stories.

**B  ▶ 2.2 Listen to the stories. Match pictures A–D with speakers 1–4.**

**C  Listen again and answer the questions.**

1  Who was angry about not getting to a meeting on time? _____

2  Who watched the news on a black and white television? _____

3  Who got up to make everyone coffee? _____

4  Who were trying to talk on their mobile phones? _____

5  Who thought that maybe what they remembered was just a dream? _____

6  Who wanted peace for everyone? _____

## GRAMMAR  narrative tenses

**2  Circle the correct option to complete the sentences.**

1  Simon was feeling exhausted because
   a) the baby wasn't sleeping all night.
   b) the baby hadn't slept all night.

2  We were driving to the hospital to visit Sam when
   a) they called to say she had gone home.
   b) they were calling to say that she was going home.

3  By the time we got to the beach
   a) the rain had stopped.
   b) the rain stopped.

4  Juan was feeling excited because
   a) he wasn't seeing his parents for ten years.
   b) he hadn't seen his parents for ten years.

5  She was singing an old folk song
   a) which I hadn't heard for years.
   b) which I didn't hear for years.

6  Everyone was dancing because
   a) Porto had just won the match.
   b) Porto were just winning the match.

**3  Complete the conversations with the correct form of the verbs in brackets.**

Conversation 1

A: What ¹_____ (happen) to you on Saturday night? We ²_____ (wait) for ages, but you ³_____ (not come).

B: I'm really sorry. I ⁴_____ (drive) back from Aga's house when my car ⁵_____ (break) down.

A: Why didn't you call?

B: My phone ⁶_____ (run out) of battery.

Conversation 2

A: ⁷_____ you _____ (enjoy) your dinner last night?

B: No. Actually, I ⁸_____ (hate) it.

A: Why? What happened?

B: Well, we ⁹_____ (book) a table, but I ¹⁰_____ (not realise) it was right by the door. People ¹¹_____ (come) in and out all evening and it was freezing. Then, when the waiter ¹²_____ (pour) my wine, he ¹³_____ (spill) it down my dress. And also, we ¹⁴_____ (order) fish, which they ¹⁵_____ (say) was fresh. But when it ¹⁶_____ (arrive) it ¹⁷_____ (taste) terrible!

## VOCABULARY the news

**4A Complete the headlines with the words in the box.**

crash demonstration attacked
strikes earthquake fugitive floods
hostages shot collapse

1. Plane _____ in the Mediterranean

2. **Thousands killed and more homeless in huge _____ in Haiti**

3. Pirates take families as _____

4. **HEAVY _____ DESTROY HOUSES AS RIVER WATER RISES**

5. _____ arrested at airport

6. **Thousands attend anti-war _____**

7. **JOURNALIST _____ AND KILLED BY GUNMAN**

8. **PRIME MINISTER _____ WITH EGGS AND ROTTEN FRUIT DURING CONFERENCE**

9. **Global economic crisis as banks and insurance companies _____**

10. **Train workers' _____ cause delays**

**B Circle the correct option to complete the sentences.**

1. We need to check our flights. The airport workers are planning _____.

   a) strikes   b) demonstrations

2. Fire officers had to clear the area in case the buildings _____.

   a) attacked   b) collapsed

3. Police were congratulated when the _____ was finally arrested.

   a) hostage   b) fugitive

4. If the rain continues, more _____ are expected.

   a) floods   b) earthquakes

5. More than 100 people were rescued when the train _____.

   a) crashed   b) shot

## WRITING a news report; time linkers

**5A Put the sentences/paragraphs in the correct order to complete three news reports, A–C. Each report should have three parts:**

1. an introductory statement to say what happened
2. background information
3. a concluding statement (or an opinion in quotes).

### REPORT A

a _____ The pupils mark their fingerprints [1]*while / as soon as* they enter the church. They will be monitored over three years.

b _____ [2]*During / Until* that time, if they attend 200 masses, they will be excused from taking one exam.

c _____ A Polish priest has installed an electronic reader in his church in Warsaw for school children to leave their fingerprints when they attend mass.

### REPORT B

a _____ But Kiyotaka Yamana, a Tokyo resident who started the 'Love Message Yelling Event' after his marriage failed, said that didn't mean they were unromantic. 'The dominant image of Japanese men is of overworked businessmen, but I wanted to tell people around the world that Japanese men are actually very romantic,' Yamana told reporters.

b _____ [3]*While / During* they are on stage, yelling 'I love you' or 'Let me be with you', they are filmed, and the event is broadcast on national television. [4]*Until / By the time* recently, Japanese men have usually chosen not to talk very openly about love.

c _____ Love is really in the air in Tokyo at the 'Love Message Yelling Event'. [5]*While / During* the event, dozens of people stand on a stage in Hibiya Park in central Tokyo and shout out love messages to their partners.

### REPORT C

a _____ However, [6]*by the time / until* they reached the ruins, the area had been cut off by floods and mudslides, and they had to wait [7]*as soon as / until* army helicopters could come and airlift them to safety.

b _____ The travellers had finished the difficult 45-km (28-mile) trek along Peru's Inca trail to see the famous Machu Picchu ruins.

c _____ Over a thousand tourists had to be evacuated from Machu Picchu last week.

**B For each report, answer the questions.**

1. What happened?
2. Where was it exactly?
3. Why did it happen?

**C Underline the correct time linkers to complete the reports.**

**D Write a short news report (80–120 words) describing a recent news event in your country.**

## VOCABULARY  *say/tell*

**1**  Complete the sentences with the correct form of *say* or *tell*.

1  President Obama _____ a joke, and everybody laughed.

2  The manager called to _____ she was sorry about what had happened.

3  I still can't believe that he _____ me such a big lie. I'm furious with him.

4  Someone once _____ me a story about that.

5  Listen. Why don't you just _____ what you mean?

6  As Jodie walked past the table, the young man looked up and _____ 'hello'.

## FUNCTION  telling a story

**2**  Underline the correct options to complete the story.

# STUCK IN THE SNOW

[1]*This happened when | All of a sudden* I was snowboarding with a few friends in Italy. [2]*Before long | Well*, most of the group were really good skiers, [3]*so | in the end* one day we went to the top of this difficult run. [4]*In the beginning | Anyway*, the field was full of fresh snow, and in the middle a tree had fallen down, and was covered in snow. It made a perfect jump, so soon everyone was queuing up to perform tricks. [5]*Well | Before long* it was my turn. Well, I went as fast as possible, and jumped up ready to do a back flip. But I forgot to bend my knees. [6]*So | The next thing I knew*, I was pointing down, like an arrow. I went head first into the snow, right up to my waist. My legs were sticking up in the air, and I couldn't move. [7]*In the end | Before long*, they had to dig me out. [8]*Anyway | All of a sudden* we've all laughed about it ever since.

## LEARN TO  keep a story going

**3**  Complete the conversation with the words in the box.

| what   Really   no   then   amazing |
| happened   Oh   kidding |

**A:**  You'll never guess what happened to Mukul.

**B:**  No. What happened?

**A:**  Well, you know he's working as a taxi driver to help pay for his medical studies.

**B:**  Yes, I know.

**A:**  Anyway, he took a family who were on holiday from Italy in his taxi. And one of his passengers was a seventy-two-year-old grandmother.

**B:**  Yes, so what [1]_____?

**A:**  Well, she left her handbag, with more than $21,000 of the family's travelling money, some very valuable jewellery, and some of their passports, in the back of his taxi.

**B:**  Oh [2]_____. You're [3]_____. So, [4]_____ did he do?

**A:**  Well, he looked in the bag to see who it belonged to.

**B:**  Yes, …

**A:**  And he found an address that was fifty miles away. So, he drove all the way there.

**B:**  And what happened [5]_____?

**A:**  Well, there was no one in …

**B:**  [6]_____ dear.

**A:**  So he left a note and his telephone number. And when the family called him, he went back and returned the bag.

**B:**  [7]_____?

**A:**  Yes. As you can imagine, the family were overjoyed, and they offered him a reward.

**B:**  How much?

**A:**  I don't know. He didn't take it. He said he couldn't accept it. He was just happy that he'd done the right thing.

**B:**  I don't believe it. That's really [8]_____.

# REVIEW AND CHECK 1: UNITS 1–2

## VOCABULARY family

**1 Complete the sentences.**

1 I recently discovered that I'm _____ to a famous football player of the 1950s.

2 There are several soldiers on my father's _____ of the family.

3 I take _____ my mother; we look very similar.

4 My _____ family consists of four grandparents, six uncles and aunts and fifteen cousins.

5 I always spend Christmas with _____ – usually my uncle, but sometimes my sister.

6 When her father died, she _____ over €10 million.

7 My great-_____ were married for twenty years before they had my grandfather!

8 We moved to Krakow fifty years ago, but my family's _____ are in Warsaw.

## GRAMMAR question forms

**2A Complete the interview questions. Use the same verbs as the answers.**

A: Who [1]_____ ?

B: I work for a small publishing company called Calinet.

A: What type of things [2]_____ ?

B: I do a lot of things – do some editing, contact authors.

A: What problems [3]_____ ?

B: I deal with problems concerning the manuscripts: mistakes, wrong length, wrong style.

A: When [4]_____ working there?

B: I started working there in 2007.

A: [5]_____ the job?

B: Yes, I do enjoy it. It's great.

A: So why [6]_____ for this job?

B: I applied because it's a great company.

**B ▶ RC1.1 Listen and repeat the questions with the correct intonation.**

## GRAMMAR review of verb tenses

**3 Put the verbs in brackets into the correct tense to complete the introduction to a speech.**

Hello, everybody! My name is Shane Towers. I [1]_____ (be) a teacher, but at the moment I [2]_____ (take) a year off to finish my Master's Degree. I [3]_____ (not start) working with children until 2005, but now I [4]_____ (love) it. Well, today I'm going to talk about Theatre of the Oppressed. I first [5]_____ (see) the name when I [6]_____ (look) through some articles for my degree. I [7]_____ (read) an article about drama in education and suddenly the name [8]_____ (jump) out at me: 'Theatre of the Oppressed'. In my country, the theatre [9]_____ (not be) usually for or about the oppressed; it's for rich or middle-class people. I [10]_____ (want) to find out more ...

## VOCABULARY relationships

**4A Match the sentences with the people in the box.**

| classmate    boss    team-mate    partner    mentor    employee    pupil    fiancée |
|---|

1 'Please finish this report for me by tomorrow morning.' _____

2 'Ian, can I borrow your pen? I forgot to write my name on my homework.' _____

3 'Come on! Together we can win this game!' _____

4 'Let's look at this together; I can give you some ideas.' _____

5 'We still need to send out the wedding invitations.' _____

6 'I have a meeting in the office with my manager at 6.00.' _____

7 'Sorry, sir. I thought we had to hand in our homework tomorrow.' _____

8 'We'll split the costs 50/50, OK?' _____

**B Mark the stress on the words in the box.**

## VOCABULARY PLUS collocations with take/get/do/go

**5 Replace _banana_ with _take_, _get_, _do_ or _go_. Use the present simple or the past simple.**

1 I _banana_ a lot of research before I _banana_ my degree. _did, got_

2 A year ago she _banana_ up a new hobby: acting. Then she _banana_ part in her first play. _____

3 Last night we _banana_ some work on the proposal and then we _banana_ for a meal. _____

4 Can you _banana_ me a favour? Can you help me to _banana_ this test? _____

5 You _banana_ after your father. I hope you don't _banana_ grey when you're twenty-five, too! _____

6 Eventually I _banana_ off Jane because she always _banana_ angry for no reason. _____

## VOCABULARY interview advice

**6 Circle the correct option to answer the questions.**

1 How should you dress before an interview?

   a) messily      b) brilliantly      c) smartly

2 How should you shake hands with someone?

   a) nicely      b) firmly      c) heavily

3 When should you arrive for an appointment?

   a) on time      b) quickly      c) late

4 What shouldn't you avoid in an interview?

   a) foot contact      b) head contact      c) eye contact

5 What should you do before an interview?

   a) some research      b) a job      c) the washing

6 What should you show in an interview?

   a) your CV      b) your photos      c) enthusiasm

## FUNCTION talking about yourself

**7** Read the conversation between Ian and his boss, John. Which lines are correct? Which have an extra word?

| | | | |
|---|---|---|---|
| I: | John, could I to ask a question? | 1 | _to_ |
| J: | Of course. What would you like to know? | 2 | ✓ |
| I: | There are but a couple of things. | 3 | _____ |
| J: | Yes, go ahead. | 4 | _____ |
| I: | I am have a query about the website. | 5 | _____ |
| J: | Yes. You know it isn't finished yet? | 6 | _____ |
| I: | Can I to ask you when it will be finished? | 7 | _____ |
| J: | It's for me, the most important thing is to get it right. | 8 | _____ |
| I: | I understand, but when will it be ready? | 9 | _____ |
| J: | I'd have really to say, websites have been a big problem for this company. | 10 | _____ |
| I: | In the my opinion, they've been the biggest problem. But when will it be ready? | 11 | _____ |
| J: | One thing I'd like for to say is that we are working hard on the website. | 12 | _____ |
| I: | So you don't have a date? | 13 | _____ |
| J: | Er … no. Sorry. | 14 | _____ |

## LEARN TO use two-word responses

**8** Put the words in the boxes into pairs to make two-word responses. Then complete the conversations with the correct responses.

| of | problem | welcome | course | no | you're |
|---|---|---|---|---|---|

1 A: Thank you so much.
  B: _____ .

2 A: Sorry about that.
  B: _____ .

3 A: Can I leave early, please?
  B: _____ .

| ahead | correct | see | I | go | you're |
|---|---|---|---|---|---|

4 A: I think the answer is 'Paris'.
  B: _____ .

5 A: Can I tell you what happened?
  B: _____ .

6 A: I couldn't come because I was ill.
  B: _____ .

| I | right | that's | please | understand | continue |
|---|---|---|---|---|---|

7 A: Is your name John Brown?
  B: _____ .

8 A: Sorry I didn't finish it.
  B: _____ .

9 A: So, I was telling you about …
  B: _____ .

## VOCABULARY types of story; the news

**9** Complete the descriptions of films with the words in the box.

| fantasy fugitive strike biopic science period earthquake collapse thriller action crash attack shot comedy |
|---|

1 This _____ describes the life of Cesar Chavez, the leader who organised a workers' _____ so that people could work under fair conditions.

2 This psychological _____ tells the story of a _____ who hides from the police while trying to prove that he is innocent.

3 This is a very funny romantic _____ that tells the story of two people who fall in love when their cars _____ on a small road.

4 This _____ fiction film describes what happens when aliens _____ Planet Earth, attempting to destroy everything.

5 This children's _____ begins when a hole opens up in the ground after an _____, and a giant, friendly creature comes out to rescue everybody.

6 This _____ drama looks at the _____ of the British Empire and what happened to those who returned to Britain from the colonies.

7 This _____ film, which begins with the President getting _____, involves two minutes of acting and ninety minutes of guns and bombs.

## GRAMMAR present perfect/past simple

**10** Read the phrases in italics and correct the ones that are wrong.

1 The Berlin Wall *has fallen* in 1989.

2 *Have you been* to any of the Caribbean islands?

3 I started work at 6a.m. but I still *haven't finished*.

4 What time *have you gone* to bed last night?

5 It's so dry here. It *hasn't rained* for weeks.

6 Did you hear about Casey? He's *broken* his leg!

7 Van Gogh *hasn't sold* many paintings during his lifetime.

8 You're a good guitar player. *Have you played* for long?

**11** ▶ RC1.2 Listen and tick the sentence you hear.

1 a) I stopped.          b) I've stopped.
2 a) We made it.         b) We've made it.
3 a) He helped me.       b) He's helped me.
4 a) They killed it.     b) They've killed it.
5 a) You worked hard.    b) You've worked hard.
6 a) I thanked her.      b) I've thanked her.

## VOCABULARY PLUS  prepositions

**12**  Complete the diary entry with the correct prepositions.

> I went ¹_____ a run in the morning while listening to some music ²_____ Eminem. I hate running ³_____ the winter, especially ⁴_____ Monday morning. It's too cold! Unfortunately, Kim is away ⁵_____ business and only gets back late ⁶_____ night, so I had to run ⁷_____ my own. It was hard work running six miles, but I did it ⁸_____ the end. Had breakfast ⁹_____ a hurry and managed to get to work ¹⁰_____ time. Problems with the bus so I went ¹¹_____ train, which was quicker. ¹²_____ chance, I heard ¹³_____ the radio that the new film ¹⁴_____ Roger Graves, an old friend of mine, was coming out ¹⁵_____ June. It's about a man who runs every morning and hates it!

## GRAMMAR  narrative tenses

**13**  Complete the sentences with the past simple, past perfect or past continuous form (positive or negative) of the verbs in the box. Use each verb once.

| turn on  finish  eat  open  do  leave  stay  listen |
|---|
| wear  go |

1  She went to Hotel Buena Vista, but I _____ in Hotel Primavera!

2  As Bilal closed the door, he realised he _____ the keys in the car.

3  Yannick _____ to music when someone knocked on the door.

4  When I got to work, I saw that I _____ one black shoe and one brown shoe!

5  When we arrived, it was cold because Dad _____ the heating.

6  Bella started the course last year, but she _____ it.

7  Goa was new to us because we _____ there before.

8  It was too hot, so I _____ the window.

9  The police want to know what you _____ between 6.30a.m. and 7.00a.m. yesterday.

10  The food tasted horrible, so we _____ it.

## VOCABULARY  say/tell

**14A**  Complete the phrases with *say* or *tell*.

1  _____ jokes

2  _____ 'hello'

3  _____ a white lie

4  _____ sorry

5  _____ stories

6  _____ what you mean

**B**  Complete the sentences with the correct form of phrases from Exercise 14A.

1  When I was young, my father always _____ before we fell asleep.

2  Most comedians _____. But his face alone makes you laugh!

3  I explained that I didn't mean to break the window! I _____!

4  She isn't very friendly, is she? She never _____ when I see her in the street.

5  He didn't want to make her cry, so instead of telling the truth, he _____.

6  Instead of talking for hours around the issue, why don't you just _____!

## FUNCTION  telling a story

**15**  Underline the correct alternatives.

A: ¹*Happened this / This happened* when I was on holiday in Portugal last year. There were three of us renting this old, scary house in the countryside. It was miles from anywhere.

B: So what ²*happened / did happen*?

A: We'd had a really nice evening. My friend is a good cook and she'd made this lovely meal, so we were feeling very content and full. ³*In anyway / Anyway*, that night, just after we'd all gone to bed, we heard this kind of scratching sound at the door. ⁴*To / In* the beginning, we just thought it was the wind and we went to sleep and forgot about it. But then the following night, the same thing: scratch, scratch at the door.

B: ⁵*But no / Oh no*!

A: ⁶*Well / Very well*, we were all in separate rooms but ⁷*after / before* long we were all sitting together in the living room, really scared. ⁸*So / So on* we talked and talked, trying to work out what to do.

B: And what ⁹*did you do / you did*?

A: ¹⁰*Final / Finally* we decided to get a knife or another weapon and go outside together to see what it was. ¹¹*The next thing / The near thing* I knew, I was at the front of three frightened girls, carrying the kitchen knife and about to unlock the front door.

B: ¹²*Dear / Oh dear*!

A: It went really quiet again. And then, all of ¹³*the sudden / a sudden*, there was the scratching sound.

B: So what ¹⁴*happened then / then happened*?

A: I opened the door and a cat jumped back and ran off into the night. All that panic and ¹⁵*for / in* the end it was just a cat!

B: That's really ¹⁶*funny / fun*!

A: Well yes, we all laughed afterwards, but it was very scary at the time!

# TEST

**Circle the correct option to complete the sentences.**

1 Sarah is _____ a famous nineteenth-century politician.

  a) related to      b) relative      c) related

2 Where _____ last summer?

  a) have you go      b) do you go      c) did you go

3 What music _____?

  a) do you listen      b) you listen to
  c) do you listen to

4 Who _____ you with this homework?

  a) helped      b) did help      c) was helped

5 _____ she like pasta?

  a) Is      b) Does      c) Do

6 I'm _____ a novel.

  a) writing      b) be writing
  c) already written

7 What _____ between 4.00p.m. and 4.30p.m.?

  a) did you do      b) were you doing
  c) you were doing

8 We are _____ of a tennis club.

  a) team-mates      b) partners      c) members

9 They _____ in a concert.

  a) did      b) took place      c) took part

10 Can you _____?

  a) make me a favour   b) do me a favour
  c) do me favour

11 You _____ your father, especially in your character.

  a) take after      b) take over      c) take to

12 I _____ research before I started the project.

  a) did a      b) took some      c) did some

13 I _____ about this topic.

  a) could question      b) ask a question
  c) have a query

14 Why don't you _____ and tell your story?

  a) go ahead      b) be ahead      c) go forward

15 _____ me, the most important thing is to be honest.

  a) By      b) For      c) According

16 I love films about the future, especially _____.

  a) fiction science      b) science fiction
  c) period drama

17 We _____ to Italy yet.

  a) didn't go      b) not have been
  c) haven't been

18 _____ Paul last night?

  a) Were you see      b) Did you see
  c) Have you seen

19 What _____ to your hair?

  a) have you done      b) you have done
  c) you did

20 I didn't want to work _____ my own.

  a) in      b) on      c) by

21 She fired the gun _____ mistake.

  a) by      b) on      c) at

22 He realised he _____ Janine before.

  a) met      b) was meeting   c) had met

23 The alarm went off while we _____.

  a) sleep      b) were sleeping
  c) had slept

24 I was nervous because I _____ a speech before.

  a) wasn't giving      b) didn't give      c) hadn't given

25 When I _____ her, she didn't know who I was.

  a) had met      b) was meeting   c) met

26 The kidnappers wanted a million dollars for each _____.

  a) hostage      b) fugitive      c) flood

27 That boy is always _____ lies.

  a) speaking      b) saying      c) telling

28 If you did something wrong, you should _____ sorry.

  a) ask      b) say      c) tell

29 All _____, the rain came down.

  a) in the end      b) very sudden   c) of a sudden

30 That's impossible – you _____ joking!

  a) must to be      b) must be      c) must

**TEST RESULT**    /30

## LISTENING

**1A** ▶ 3.1 **Listen to three people talking about their future plans. Who talks about:**

a) their university studies? _____

b) a holiday? _____

c) their weekend? _____

Kieron

Amber

Ruth

**B Listen again and circle the correct option.**

1  Where is the hostel where Ruth is planning to stay?

a) near the mountains

b) near one of the biggest lakes

c) not far from the sea

2  How far is she planning to walk each day?

a) 10–20 km     b) 20–30 km     c) 30–40 km

3  What does she plan to do in the evenings?

a) go out to a restaurant and meet other walkers

b) write about the walks they have done

c) have something to eat and go to bed

4  What is Kieron going to study at university?

a) Sports     b) Law     c) History

5  Where is he going to live? Why?

a) In a house with friends because it's fun.

b) In university accommodation because it's cheaper.

c) With his parents because they live near the university.

6  What clubs does he hope to join?

a) a wine-tasting club     b) an adventure club

c) a sports/rugby club

7  Where is Amber going for her honeymoon?

a) the Red Sea     b) the Nile     c) the Pyramids

8  What does Amber enjoy about travelling?

a) speaking to people in a different language

b) learning about a new culture

c) new experiences, meeting new people, going to new places

9  What does she plan to do while she is on holiday?

a) a scuba-diving course     b) sightseeing

c) swimming and sunbathing

**C Match the underlined phrases in sentences 1–5 with meanings a)–e).**

1  We meet up <u>every now and again</u> for walking holidays.

2  It's not everyone's idea of fun, I know, but <u>I can't wait</u>.

3  <u>To start with</u>, I'm going to stay in the university.

4  I'll have to <u>see how it goes</u>.

5  We're staying in a <u>luxury</u> hotel.

a) in the beginning

b) see what happens

c) very comfortable and expensive

d) I'm looking forward to it very much / I'm very excited

e) occasionally

## GRAMMAR the future (plans)

**2 Circle the correct options to complete the conversation.**

A: [1]_____ anywhere this weekend?

B: Yes, we [2]_____ up to Edinburgh to see some of the sights.

A: That's nice. Where [3]_____ to stay?

B: I don't know yet. I [4]_____ a look online later.

A: I've got some friends in Edinburgh. They [5]_____ have some space. I [6]_____ you their number.

B: Thanks. That's great. What about you? [7]_____ anything exciting?

A: No, I think I [8]_____ the weekend watching DVDs.

1  a) Do you go          b) Are you going

2  a) 're going          b) 'll go

3  a) are you going      b) might you

4  a) have              b) 'm going to have

5  a) might             b) are going to

6  a) 'll give          b) 'm going to give

7  a) Do you do         b) Are you doing

8  a) 'll spend         b) 'm spending

**3 Complete the email. Use the present continuous, *will/might* or *be going to*. There may be more than one possibility.**

Hi Ros – [1]_____ (you/do) anything at the weekend? Do you want to come out with us? Danny and I [2]_____ (go/out) on Saturday night. It would be great if you could come. We [3]_____ (try) one of the restaurants in Trastevere – it's really nice round there.

One thing we've planned is we [4]_____ (meet) up with a few people from the course for a drink first, in Piazza Santa Maria. Do you know it? We [5]_____ (be) outside Café Marzo from about 6.30, if you want to join us. I'm not sure how late we [6]_____ (be). If anyone still has enough energy at the end of the evening, a DJ friend of mine [7]_____ (play) at the Gioia Music Restaurant, so we [8]_____ (go) there and dance a bit afterwards. We'll see how things go. I [9]_____ (call) you tomorrow to see what your plans are.

Speak soon,

Silvia

**4A** ▶ 3.2 **Listen to the sentences. Which words are stressed? Circle the option you hear.**

1 a) They're <u>going</u> to <u>play</u> <u>squash</u>.
  b) <u>They</u>'re going to play <u>squash</u>.

2 a) I'm <u>going</u> to buy a <u>new</u> <u>phone</u>.
  b) I'm going to <u>buy</u> a new <u>phone</u>.

3 a) She's <u>going</u> to <u>spend</u> a week in <u>Greece</u>.
  b) She's going to spend a <u>week</u> in <u>Greece</u>.

4 a) He isn't <u>going</u> to eat <u>anything</u>.
  b) He <u>isn't</u> going to <u>eat</u> anything.

5 a) Are you <u>going</u> to <u>walk</u> to the <u>station</u>?
  b) Are <u>you</u> going to <u>walk</u> to the station?

6 a) <u>He's</u> going to change his <u>job</u>.
  b) He's going to <u>change</u> his <u>job</u>.

**B** **Listen again and repeat. Focus on the pronunciation of *going to* in fast speech.**

## VOCABULARY communication

**5** **Use the clues to complete the crossword.**

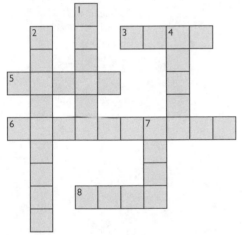

**Across**

3 Talk in a friendly and informal way

5 Talk too proudly about something that you have, or that you have done

6 Say something nice to someone in order to praise them, for example about their appearance or about how well they have done something

8 Tell someone that something dangerous or bad may happen, so they can avoid it or prevent it

**Down**

1 Talk or write about other people's behaviour or private lives

2 Say that you are sorry about something you have done or said

4 Shout and say angry things to someone because you disagree

7 Complain about something in an annoying way

## WRITING messages; using note form

**6A** **Match messages 1–6 with situations a)–f).**

1 Gone to lunch. Back soon.

2 Mr Jackson called. No message. Will call again later.

3 Dentist appointment cancelled. Need to rebook.

4 At the cinema. Dinner in the oven. See you later.

5 Messages — Going swimming after school – want to come?

6 Sorry, didn't tidy bedroom – was late for school.

a) a brother leaving a message for his sister
b) a mother leaving a message for her son
c) a secretary leaving a message for his/her boss
d) a colleague leaving a message for other colleagues
e) a son leaving a message for his mother
f) a person leaving a message for self as a reminder

**B** **Which words have been deliberately left out of the messages? Rewrite the messages in full.**

1 _____

2 _____

3 _____

4 _____

5 _____

6 _____

**C** **Write notes for these situations.**

1 To your boss: Tell him that Mr Ali telephoned, and that you have arranged for them to meet at Mr Ali's office tomorrow morning at 9a.m.

2 To your brother: Invite him out to the cinema this evening.

3 To your colleague: Say that you have gone home and will be back in the office tomorrow.

## READING

**1 Read the text and choose the best heading.**

a Five Ways to Find ET*    b Man and ET: A Communication Breakdown?    c Music in Space

*ET means extraterrestrial – a non-human, intelligent lifeform that may exist on other planets.

In 1977, Man sent a shuttle (a type of spaceship) called *Voyager 2* into space. The idea was to communicate with extraterrestrial life. In the space shuttle there was a recording specially made to introduce humanity to any aliens who found the shuttle. The recording contained the word *hello* in many languages, the sounds of a baby crying and a couple kissing, a message of peace from the Secretary General of the United Nations, and music from all over the world: Mexican mariachis, panpipes from Peru, a Japanese shakuhachi piece, even a song by Chuck Berry. One TV programme imagined that aliens found *Voyager 2*, listened to the music and sent a message back to humanity: 'Send more Chuck Berry!' [1]_____

For as long as Man has looked at the sky, we have wondered if there is intelligent life in space. In 1984, the SETI (Search for Extraterrestrial Intelligence) Institute was founded. One of its main tasks is sending signals into space in the hope that an intelligent alien life form will make contact. In other words, SETI is doing what *Voyager 2* did, but with 150 full-time scientists, educators and other staff working from sunny California on Planet Earth.

SETI has spent millions of dollars, and used up decades of people's working lives. And still nothing. So the big question: Why are we still waiting for a response? [2]_____

- There is no other intelligent lifeform out there. We are alone in the universe.
- There is intelligent life out there, but it communicates differently. While we use radio waves, maybe the aliens use something we don't know about.
- There is intelligent life out there, but it doesn't want to communicate with us. And who can blame it? Just look at Man's history and how we treat newly-discovered civilisations. When we are not giving them our diseases, we enslave them, steal their land and get them addicted to junk food and bad TV. And now we want to say 'hello' to another species? [3]_____
- We have not searched for long enough or far enough. Man has only been looking for ET for three or four decades. That is a tiny amount of time compared to the age of the universe. [4]_____
- We have succeeded in communicating with extraterrestrials, but government organisations are hiding this information from the public.
This is the conspiracy theorists' dream; somewhere in an underground bunker (usually thought to be in Roswell, New Mexico, USA), there are crashed UFOs and the bodies of dead aliens being examined by secret government agencies. But no one has any evidence of an alien. [5]_____

**2 Read the text again and answer the questions.**

1 What was the purpose of *Voyager 2*?

_____

2 Which word was chosen for the recording, and spoken in different languages?

_____

3 How does SETI try to communicate with extraterrestrials?

_____

4 Who works for SETI?

_____

5 How long have we been looking for extraterrestrials?

_____

6 What do conspiracy theorists think?

_____

**3 These sentences have been taken out of the text in Exercise 1. Where should they go? Write the letter in the correct gap 1–5.**

a Even in our own communities, we kill animals, murder each other, and ruin the environment.

b And no one has found the secret bunker either.

c Space is also rather big, and we haven't searched very much of it.

d There are a number of possible answers.

e It may be a good joke, but in reality, after over thirty years we are still waiting for a response.

**4 Find words or phrases in the text to match definitions 1–4.**

1 form of energy that moves through the air, allowing us to send and receive messages (lines 26–28) _____

2 to make someone a slave (lines 29–34) _____

3 a group of animals or plants of the same kind (lines 29–34) _____

4 a strongly built room under the ground (lines 39–46) _____

## VOCABULARY future time markers

**5A** Complete the predictions with the words in the box.

term  next  future  in  time  short  from  ~~shortly~~

1 I'm going to find out my exam results _shortly_ . Then I hope to go to university.

2 In the near _____ I'm going to travel around Europe. I just need to save a bit more money.

3 The economy is weak now, but it will improve in the long _____ .

4 In the _____ term we expect our sales profits to increase by about 3 percent.

5 I'm planning to get married to my boyfriend _____ a year or two. Then we'll start a family.

6 I have no idea where I'll be a long time _____ now, but it won't be in a big city.

7 In ten years' _____ I hope to be a doctor working with children somewhere in Africa.

8 I'm starting a new job _____ month. If all goes well, I'll keep working for the company until I retire.

**B** Which predictions are about things that will happen soon? Which are about things that will happen more than three years in the future?

## GRAMMAR the future (predictions)

**6** Rewrite the second sentence so that it has the same meaning as the first sentence. Use the words in capitals.

1 There's a possibility that I will study in Spain. MAY
_I may study in Spain_ .

2 Where do you plan to stay? WILL
Where _____ ?

3 Will you speak to Ted tomorrow? GOING
Are _____ ?

4 Janine probably won't pass her exam. UNLIKELY
Janine _____ .

5 The weather forecast predicts a storm. GOING
There's _____ .

6 He has a chance of becoming the champion. COULD
He _____ .

7 Scientists will probably find a cure for cancer one day. LIKELY
Scientists _____ .

8 I don't think we'll be able to attend the meeting. MAY
We _____ .

9 There isn't time for us to go shopping. WON'T
We _____ .

10 There's an opportunity to meet next week. COULD
We _____ .

**7** Complete the text with one word in each gap. Contractions are one word.

### THE FUTURE OF LANGUAGE LEARNING

In the future we [1]_____ going to see more and more people using technology to learn languages. There will [2]_____ software that gets computers to read texts aloud and translate them. And we [3]_____ only talk on the computer; we will also talk with the computer in any language we choose.

We will also begin to understand the importance of the five senses in language education, and researchers and publishers are likely [4]_____ look at children's toys for inspiration. Music is going [5]_____ play an increasing role in language learning. Short texts and phrases will be set to music and this will help students to remember the words, just as *The A, B, C Song* helps children learn the alphabet.

Textbooks may [6]_____ unrecognisable when compared to today's books. They will come with microchips that produce smells and sounds. So if we are learning the word *bread*, when we touch that part of the page it will smell of bread. If we are learning the word *cry*, when we touch the word it [7]_____ make a crying sound.

At first, these books [8]_____ likely to be expensive, but market economics will drive prices down. So get ready for fun and games while you learn another language – these changes could happen sooner than you think!

## VOCABULARY PLUS idioms

**8** Underline the correct alternatives.

1 'I'm no good at [1]big / _small_ talk. I always put my [2]*foot / hand* in it, and it's really not my cup of [3]*tea / coffee*.

2 'I joined the [4]*mouse / rat* race last year when I became a project manager. I have to keep my [5]*ear / eye* on three or four projects at the same time. We're always [6]*working / running* against the clock, and quite often we [7]*work / run* out of time.'

3 'I thought an online course would be a [8]*piece / bit* of cake, but I soon found myself in [9]*cold / hot* water. It was really difficult. I told one of the other students what was on my [10]*mind / brain*. He was an A student, and he gave me a [11]*foot / hand* with one of the assignments and I passed the course.'

## FUNCTION dealing with misunderstandings

**1** ▶ 3.3 Cover Exercise 2. Listen and match pictures A–D with conversations 1–4.

**2** Listen again and complete the conversations.

**Conversation 1**

A: The living room is too green and the floor's all wrong.

B: Sorry?

A: The living room. Green. And I hate the floor.

B: You've [1]_____ me.

A: I'm talking about Mum's new house. I don't like the colour of the walls in the living room.

B: Oh!

**Conversation 2**

A: Hello? I'm trying to find my lost luggage.

B: Ah, OK.

A: My bags went missing in Montevideo in Uruguay, after a flight from Curitiba, Brazil.

B: [2]_____ you say that [3]_____ ? Montevideo?

A: I flew from Curitiba to Montevideo and my bags went missing.

B: Have you reported it already?

A: Yes, the name is Anders Kleeburg.

B: Hang on. Could you [4]_____ the last name? Anders … ?

A: Kleeburg. K-l-e-e-b-u-r-g.

**Conversation 3**

A: OK, so cricket. So this is the bowler, OK? He runs up and bowls at the batsman.

B: [5]_____ exactly do you [6]_____ ? What's a bowler?

A: A bowler is the person with the ball in his hand, OK? And he tries to get the batsman out. Get him off the field.

B: Do you mean to [7]_____ he tries to kill the batsman with the ball?

A: No!

**Conversation 4**

A: Did you read this?! About popcorn. In 1948, two American scientists found some popcorn in a cave in New Mexico and dated it. It was over five thousand years old.

B: I didn't [8]_____ any of that. Are you talking about popcorn?

A: Yeah, it's an ancient food. Popcorn is thousands of years old.

B: I don't [9]_____ what you're [10]_____ . You mean the popcorn we ate in the cinema yesterday is thousands of years old!

A: No! Popcorn in general. People have eaten it for thousands of years.

## LEARN TO reformulate

**3** Put B's words in the correct order to complete the conversations.

**Conversation 1**

A: I'm afraid you have to wear a tie in this nightclub.

B: we / can't / saying / in / you're / so / come

_____

**Conversation 2**

A: The show starts at nine o'clock.

B: you / at / it / starts / didn't / ten / o'clock / say?

_____

**Conversation 3**

A: The pass mark for this exam is seventy percent.

B: what / failed / mean / so / we / you / is

_____

**Conversation 4**

A: This type of car is twice as expensive as the other one.

B: me / do / costs / to / that / tell / you / it / mean / €50,000?

_____

**Conversation 5**

A: No other team can catch us.

B: the / words, / we / in / are / other / champions

_____

## VOCABULARY personal qualities

**1A Complete the words about personal qualities.**

1 He won the election because he is a g_____
  c_____. People enjoy listening to him talk.

2 Susan's h_____-w_____ nature helped her
  through university, when she had to study a lot.

3 Sami's very l_____. He doesn't work hard at shool,
  and he doesn't help at home, either.

4 Tim started at the bottom of the company, but he was
  a_____. He knew that one day he would be the
  manager of the whole organisation.

5 Lucy's a very g_____ l_____. She listens to
  people, and then decides what's best for everyone to do.

6 He hates to lose a race. He's very c_____.

7 I find it difficult to make decisions. I'm a bit i_____.

8 You need to be more creative and think o_____
  t_____ b_____.

9 They are a group of very m_____ students. They
  are keen to work hard.

10 Being a racing driver, Anton has to be a r_____
  t_____. He isn't afraid of danger.

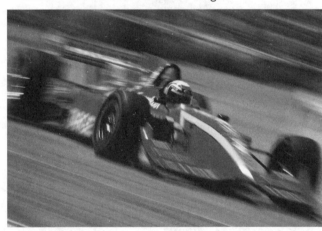

**B Find words or phrases in Exercise 1A which have the
opposite meaning to 1–8.**

1 makes decisions easily *indecisive*

2 not interested in competing with others _____

3 lazy _____

4 needs someone else to make them work _____

5 doesn't communicate well _____

6 not good at organising a team of people _____

7 doesn't like dangerous situations _____

8 not interested in becoming successful _____

## GRAMMAR must, have to, should (obligation)

**2 Match sentences 1–8 with sentences a)–h). Then
underline the correct alternative.**

1 We *don't have to / shouldn't* wear a uniform at work.

2 You *shouldn't / have to* stay up all night studying.

3 I think you *should / mustn't* talk to your boss.

4 You *don't have to / mustn't* drink and drive.

5 I think he *mustn't / should* start his own company.

6 Nurses *have to / should* work long hours.

7 You *don't have to / mustn't* cheat during the exam.

8 I *must / don't have to* leave at 4 o'clock.

9 You *should / don't have to* apologise for his behaviour.

10 We *should / must* remember to book the tickets today.

a) He's very ambitious.

b) You need to find out why he shouted at you.

c) It wasn't your fault.

d) You'll be thrown out of the college.

e) We can wear whatever we want.

f) It'll be too late if we wait until tomorrow.

g) It's against the law.

h) Otherwise I'll miss my train.

i) You'll be too tired tomorrow.

j) It's no good if you want a nine-to-five job.

**3 Correct one mistake in each sentence.**

1 You must ~~to~~ tell him as soon as possible.

2 I've finished this exercise. What I should do now?

3 The clients don't has to come to the office. We can meet
  them at the restaurant.

4 I shouldn't to tell you this, but the boss is leaving on
  Monday.

5 Do we have wear a uniform?

6 Everybody must leaving the building by 6p.m.

7 She have to be at work by 7.30a.m.

8 I think you should to check what time the film starts.

9 You don't must use a mobile phone in the classroom.

10 We have wait until the IT man comes to fix the system.

## LISTENING

**4A** Look at the pictures. What qualities do you think are important for these jobs?

 A

 B

 C

 D

 E

 F

**B** ▶ 4.1 Listen to six people talking about their jobs. Match pictures A–F above with speakers 1–6.

**C** Listen again. Who says these things? Write the number of the speaker next to each statement.

1 You have to be organised, and have a good memory, too.
2 And you need to pay attention to detail.
3 You shouldn't get stressed too easily.
4 You have to care about the people you're looking after.
5 You always have to be on time.
6 And you have to be able to work well under pressure.
7 You must be very accurate and observant.  *1*
8 You have to be able to stay calm.

## VOCABULARY PLUS confusing words

**5A** Complete the conversations with the words in the box.

| job work remember remind forget leave hear listen fun funny won earn |
| --- |

1 A: Oh no, _____ to that. It's raining and I don't have an umbrella.
　 B: Why not? Did you _____ it at home?
　 A: Yes, I did.
　 B: Here. Use mine.

2 A: Can you _____ me to post that letter on the way home?
　 B: Sure. Just _____ to bring it with you.

3 A: Did you have a good night last night?
　 B: Yes, it was really _____. We danced until two in the morning, but today I feel terrible.

4 A: I got the _____, by the way.
　 B: Congratulations! That's brilliant news.
　 A: Yes, I'm so excited. Finally, I'm going to _____ a proper salary.
　 B: That's great. Well done.

5 A: I've got to go to _____ now. I'll see you later.
　 B: Yes, don't _____ we're meeting Chaz at 7.30.
　 A: Don't worry. I'll be there.

6 A: Did you _____ the joke about the scarecrow?
　 B: No.
　 A: He _____ an award for being outstanding in his field.
　 B: That's not even _____.

**B** Complete the sentences with words from Exercise 5A.

1 Can you _____ me to call my brother later? It's his birthday.
2 Did you _____ about that couple who _____ millions of pounds on the Euro lottery?
3 I don't get paid enough. I need to get a new _____.
4 We're having a meeting tomorrow morning. Don't _____!
5 I really enjoy my _____. I find it interesting, and the people I work with are good _____.
6 He's so _____. He always makes me laugh.

# DREAM JOB TURNS INTO NIGHTMARE

1. It was advertised as the best job in the world. And it certainly looked good. You would be paid ($189,000 for six months) to surf, sail, and swim. The job came with a beachside mansion, with its own swimming pool, and fantastic views of the ocean. All you had to do was look after tiny Hamilton Island, situated off the coast of Queensland. Duties included feeding the fish, and writing a blog of your experiences to help encourage tourism in the area. There were more than 34,000 applicants for the job from all over the world, so Ben Southall was delighted when he beat them all, and won the contract.

2. But, as it turned out, it wasn't quite the dream job that some people might have expected. Firstly, it was incredibly busy. Ben found himself working seven days a week, and up to nineteen hours a day. He had a busy schedule of events to attend, with promotional events, press conferences, training courses and administrative duties. 'It has been very busy, busier than most people would have imagined, and certainly busier than I had imagined,' Mr Southall told reporters when he finished his contract.

3. In fact, during his six months, Ben visited ninety 'exotic locations', made forty-seven video diaries, and gave more than 250 media interviews – including a chat with popular US TV host Oprah Winfrey. He also posted more than 75,000 words in sixty separate blogs, uploaded more than 2,000 photos, and 'tweeted' more than 730 times.

4. That didn't leave much time for surfing, sailing or simply relaxing and enjoying the sea views. And when he did get the chance to try out his water sports, things didn't always go well. On one trip, Ben was stung by a deadly jellyfish. The Irukandji jellyfish are transparent and very small, so they are very difficult to see in the water.

5. 'I was enjoying a post-Christmas jetski session with some friends at a quiet beach on Hamilton Island and as I climbed off the back of the ski and onto the beach, felt a small bee-like sting on my forearm,' Mr Southall wrote on his blog. Within thirty minutes, Ben was feeling the venom. He was hot and sweaty, with headaches and pains in his chest, and high blood pressure. Ben had to be rushed to a doctor who diagnosed the symptoms and gave him some medication. Luckily, Ben was fine, but it was an unwelcome end to his stay in paradise. On the blog he wrote, 'This was not what I'd wanted at all – I'm supposed to be relaxing in my last few days on Hamilton Island.' Ben was lucky to survive.

6. However, he still insists that he enjoyed himself immensely. In fact, Tourism Queensland is offering him a new contract, and he will also write a book about his experiences.

## READING

**1A** Ben Southall got a 'dream job': looking after Hamilton Island, off the coast of Queensland, Australia. This article describes how the job turned into a nightmare. Which of these problems do you think it will mention?

> loneliness   free time   feeling bored   other
> money   illness   problems with animals

**B** Read the article to see if you were right. Then answer the questions.

1 What three things help to make the job 'the best job in the world'?

2 Why was the job not as 'ideal' as it seemed at first?

3 What happened to Ben towards the end of his contract?

4 What is he going to do now?

**2** Tick the things which Ben did as part of his job.

1 gave speeches

2 made video diaries

3 managed a big team of people

4 gave interviews

5 attended press conferences

6 learned a new language

7 met politicians

8 wrote a novel

9 wrote a blog about his experiences

10 learned to surf and sail

**3** Find words or phrases in the text to match definitions 1–8.

1 a large house by the sea (paragraph 1) _____

2 a plan that includes a lot of things to be done in a short time (paragraph 2) _____

3 meetings at which someone answers questions asked by people from newspapers, television, etc. (paragraph 2) _____

4 activities involved in managing the work of a company or organisation (paragraph 2) _____

5 posted a comment using the website Twitter (paragraph 3) _____

6 have an opportunity (paragraph 4) _____

7 taken very quickly (paragraph 5) _____

8 very, very much (paragraph 6) _____

## VOCABULARY strong adjectives

**4** Complete the sentences with the correct word.

1 a) I thought the show was *brilliant / boiling*.

  b) Is the heating on? It's *brilliant / boiling* in here.

2 a) Have you heard the news? Isn't it *terrible / furious*?

  b) All the trains were delayed. I was *terrible / furious*.

3 a) I'd invite you round, but my apartment is *delicious / tiny*.

  b) Have you tried these salads? They're *delicious / tiny*.

4 a) I can't do it – it's *exhausted / impossible*!

  b) I'm going home. I'm *exhausted / impossible*.

5 a) It's a *fascinating / huge* book about naval history.

  b) $50,000! That's a *fascinating / huge* amount of money!

## GRAMMAR *used to, would*

**5** Complete the paragraphs. Use one word for each gap.

> I used ¹_____ work for a big company. I ²_____ to work long hours and I ³_____ dream of living in a more exotic location, sitting on a beach with my laptop. Now I run my own website business. I don't earn as much money as I ⁴_____ to earn, but I'm much happier.

> I ⁵_____ to work as a computer programmer. Most of the time, I ⁶_____ enjoy it. But I didn't ⁷_____ to like being in an office all day. So, I decided to get a job working outdoors. Now, I train people in forestry skills, so I'm outside most of the time. And my lifestyle is much healthier than it ⁸_____ to be.

**6A** Rewrite the sentences with *used to*.

1 Did you spend your holidays by the sea?

_____

2 We didn't have a dog when I was a child.

_____

3 Daniel was one of the naughtiest boys in the class, but he's much better now.

_____

4 I loved reading in the evening, but now I'm too tired.

_____

5 I remember how I sat in my grandfather's studio and watched him paint.

_____

6 I was quite fat. Then, I went on a diet and lost ten kilos.

_____

7 Children always played around on the streets in the old days, but there's nobody here now.

_____

8 They lived in a big house, but they had to move.

_____

**B** Tick the sentences in Exercise 6A where you could replace *used to* with *would*.

**7A** Look at the underlined words. Are they pronounced with a /s/ or /z/ sound?

1 I <u>used</u> to be very sporty.

2 Can I <u>use</u> your phone?

3 He never <u>used</u> to worry about it.

4 I <u>used</u> to live in USA when I was 18.

5 This stuff is <u>used</u> to kill insects.

6 I don't <u>use</u> the car much any more.

7 We <u>used</u> to love going there on holiday.

8 I didn't <u>use</u> to live in Europe.

**B** ▶ 4.2 Listen and check. Then listen and repeat. Focus on the pronunciation of /juːstə/.

## WRITING a letter; organising your ideas

**8A** Put the parts of the covering letter in the correct order.

> _____ Thank you for your consideration. If you require any further information, please do not hesitate to contact me. I can be reached at vinniej22@dmail.com or 07788 922 123. I look forward to hearing from you ¹<u>soon</u>.
>
> _1_ Dear Ms Nelson,
>
> _____ I believe that my communication skills, customer service abilities, and positive work ethic would make me an asset to the shop.
>
> _____ I am currently studying English at Exeter University and I am looking for summer work to help me finance my studies. ²<u>I think I would be good at this job.</u> Firstly, I am both hard-working and organised, and I have excellent communication skills. Secondly, I have ³<u>shown that I am good at</u> customer service. In my previous job, on the reception desk at Queen's Hospital, I had ⁴<u>practical</u> experience of providing quality customer service, and working with all types of people.
>
> _____ Yours sincerely,
>
> _____ I am writing to you ⁵<u>about</u> the summer position at SunnySam's Electronics, advertised on www.summerjobs4students.com. ⁶<u>I want to apply</u> for the post. I attach my CV, application form and all the information required in the advertisement.
>
> _____ Vinnie Jessop

**B** Replace the underlined sections 1–6 in the letter with the phrases in the box. Write the correct number.

> hands-on _____    at your earliest convenience _____
> regarding _____    proven ability at _____
> I would like to submit an application _____
> I believe I meet all the requirements of the post _____

**C** Write a covering letter (120–180 words) for a summer job working as a restaurant/shop manager.

## VOCABULARY business

**1A** Circle the correct options to complete the text.

Hi Lucy,

I'm just writing to tell you about my new job. Remember when I had to ¹_____ for ²_____ last month? Well, I got the job. I'm so pleased about it, because in my last job I worked for a really difficult ³_____, but things here are much better. The people in the office are really good fun, and we work well as a ⁴_____. My new boss is a ⁵_____ businessman, who ⁶_____ a six-figure ⁷_____! But he's very generous with his money, and takes us out to lunch every week. The only problem now is that I still arrive late for work all the time. I hope I don't get ⁸_____.

Let me know how you're getting on at work. Speak soon.

Becca

| | | | |
|---|---|---|---|
| 1 | a) be | b) go | c) make |
| 2 | a) an interview | b) a job | c) a work |
| 3 | a) colleague | b) job | c) boss |
| 4 | a) team | b) salary | c) businessman |
| 5 | a) difficult | b) successful | c) six-figure |
| 6 | a) works | b) is | c) earns |
| 7 | a) job | b) salary | c) money |
| 8 | a) interview | b) boss | c) fired |

IT MIGHT BE BETTER IF WE WORK AS A TEAM

**B** Use the phrases in Exercise 1A to complete the sentences.

1 He's not easy to work for. He's a very _____ _____.

2 They were surprised to find out that the tramp was actually a _____ _____.

3 I like the people in the office. We _____ well as a _____.

4 They're looking for a new manager, so I'm going to _____ for an _____ next week.

5 We don't _____ a _____-_____ salary, but we really enjoy the job.

6 Unless you change your attitude, you will soon _____ _____.

## FUNCTION reaching agreement

**2** Complete the conversation with the phrases in the box.

not sure that I agree   suggest we think about
see what you mean   see things   that's a good idea
How about if we   That's fine

A: The way I ¹_____, the first thing we need to do is update the website.

B: Yes, ²_____. But we haven't decided what information to put there.

A: I know. I ³_____ what should be on the site, and then decide who's going to work on it.

B: ⁴_____ by me.

C: I'm ⁵_____, actually. I think we need to look at the finances first. We don't know how much money we can spend on the website yet.

B: I ⁶_____, but I'm not sure what to do. ⁷_____ decide what we would like first, and then look at how much it will cost?

A: Fine. That sounds good to me.

## LEARN TO manage a discussion

**3** Complete the sentences with the words in the box.

on (x2)   all   recap   to   up

1 Let's focus _____ the main problems, and talk about the rest if we have time.

2 OK, but first of _____, we need to look at the notes from the last meeting.

3 Moving _____ to the next point. What are we going to do about salaries?

4 So, let's _____ on the main ideas we've discussed, and then we'll stop for lunch.

5 I think we need to come back _____ the decision to relocate.

6 Let's sum _____ what we've talked about.

## GRAMMAR the future (plans)

**1 Circle the correct option to complete the sentences.**

1 I'm _____ out with Aleks on Friday night.
  a) going
  b) go
  c) might go

2 _____ married in May.
  a) Are we going get
  b) We're going to getting
  c) We're going to get

3 This film is boring. I think _____ to bed.
  a) I'm to going
  b) I'll go
  c) I might going

4 _____ going to do anything special at the weekend?
  a) You are
  b) Are you
  c) Do you

5 Great idea! _____ have a party to celebrate.
  a) We'll
  b) We going to
  c) We're having to

6 Who _____ invite?
  a) will you
  b) will you going to
  c) you might

7 Peter _____ fifty on Saturday!
  a) is being
  b) is going to be
  c) might be

8 _____ a Thai curry. I'm expecting about twenty people.
  a) I'm going to cook
  b) I will to cook
  c) I'm cooking

## VOCABULARY communication; future time markers

**2 Complete the sentences with the correct word.**

1 a) She likes to *chat / apologise* to friends on the phone.
  b) I really think you should *chat / apologise* for what you have done.

2 a) He's always *warning / moaning* about things: the weather, the economy, the government.
  b) You can't say that I didn't *warn / moan* you. I told you he would be angry.

3 a) When you're stressed, you are more likely to *gossip / argue* about silly things, like who does the washing-up.
  b) They like to go out in the evening and *gossip / argue* about other friends, and what they're doing.

4 a) He *boasted / complimented* me on the dress I was wearing.
  b) She likes to *boast / compliment* about how much money she earns and how she is the best at her job.

5 a) We'll be leaving *shortly / near*.
  b) I can't see him leaving his job in the *shortly / near* future.

6 a) We'd like to buy our own house in a *term / year* or two.
  b) In the long *term / year*, I think she made the right decision.

7 a) I'd like to start my own business at some point in the future, but that will be a *short / long* time from now.
  b) In the *short / long* term, over the next few weeks, we want to see business improve.

8 a) In ten *next / years'* time, I hope to be a surgeon.
  b) *Next / Years'* month, we will celebrate twenty years of marriage.

## GRAMMAR the future (predictions)

**3 Underline the correct alternative to complete the text.**

### THE FUTURE OF FREE MUSIC

So, with everybody downloading music on the internet for free, what is the future of the music industry? We asked some music experts for their opinions.

**Matthew G – head of Indit Records, UK**
'Basically, I think things [1]*aren't likely to / are going to* change very much. People [2]*may / might not* like it, but governments [3]*may / aren't going to* introduce more laws to punish people who steal music by downloading it for free. And this [4]*is going to / isn't going to* force people to move to music download sites where you pay for your music. It's already happening, and I think in the future this process [5]*won't to / is likely to* continue.'

**Ian M – music reporter**
'I think the future [6]*will / is likely* look very different. People [7]*couldn't / won't* pay for every track which they listen to any more. I think they [8]*are going / may* use a subscription site, so they pay a monthly fee and then can download as much music as they want to listen to, legally. I think we [9]*are going to / may not* see more and more record companies begin to use services like this. There [10]*could / couldn't* also be social networking sites, where people pay to join and then they can listen to each other's music.'

## VOCABULARY PLUS idioms

**4** Write the second sentence so that it means the same as the first. Use idioms which include the words in capitals.

1 It's so easy.   CAKE

It's _____.

2 He was in trouble.     WATER

He was _____.

3 I said something really inappropriate.     FOOT

I put _____.

4 It's an issue which is very important to me.     HEART

It's an issue which is _____.

5 He left his job in the city to go and become a coffee farmer.  RAT

He decided to leave _____ and become a coffee farmer.

6 Could you help me sort out these papers?     HAND

Could you _____ sorting out these papers?

7 I think about her all the time.   MIND

She's always _____.

8 I don't really like R&B music.    TEA

R&B music isn't _____.

9 I like to follow what's happening in politics.     EYE

I like to _____ what's happening in politics.

10 I'm afraid we have no more time.     RUN

I'm afraid we've _____.

## FUNCTION dealing with misunderstandings; reformulate

**5** Complete the conversations with the words in the box.

| saying   mean   catch   get   other   repeat   what   say   exactly   lost |

1 A: The picture dates back to the sixteenth century when it was …

B: I didn't _____ any of that.

2 A: So, you take the third turning on the right, go straight on for 200 metres, turn left, take the first right again, and it's straight in front of you.

B: I'm sorry. You've _____ me.

3 A: If you don't have a pink stripe on your ticket, then I'm afraid staff are not allowed to let you in.

B: Apologies, but I'm afraid I don't _____ what you're saying.

4 A: We had a very minor incident involving your new car.

B: What _____ do you mean?

5 A: We are sorry to report that all trains have been cancelled.

B: Do you _____ to say we can't travel today?

6 A: I've come to collect a parcel for Mr Wainwright.

B: Can you _____ that again?

7 A: There's one stop-over, for twenty-four hours, in Bahrain.

B: Could you _____ the last thing you said?

8 A: This desk is now closed.

B: So, you're _____ that we need to move to another desk?

9 A: I'm afraid you need to vacate the premises.

B: So _____ you mean is we need to go?

10 A: We anticipate inconveniences along the route.

B: In _____ words, we're going to be late.

## VOCABULARY review

**6** Complete the words in the sentences.

1 He always wants to win. He's very co_____.

2 Part of being a good le_____ is being able to listen to people.

3 It's one of the most am_____ films I've ever seen. It's very moving.

4 I have to go to bed as soon as possible. I'm absolutely ex_____.

5 To be a successful entrepreneur, you need to be a ri_____ ta_____.

6 It's minus ten degrees outside. It's fr_____!

7 It's a fa_____ story, really interesting. It's about a man who …

8 I love my job, but I should be earning a much bigger sa_____.

9 He was always telling the bo_____ what to do, and in the end, he got fi_____.

10 I'm very nervous, because I've got to go for this job in_____ tomorrow.

11 I can't believe how angry he was. He was absolutely fu_____.

12 I'm sure she'll do well in her new job. She's very ha_____-wo_____.

**7A** Put the words in the box into the correct place in the table according to the stress pattern.

| ~~amazing~~   ~~salary~~   tasty   competitive successful   leader   interview   furious delicious   boiling   difficult   freezing exhausted   impossible |

| oOo<br>*amazing* | Ooo<br>*salary* |
|---|---|
|  |  |
| Oo | oOoo |
|  |  |

**B** ▶ RC2.1 Listen and check.

## GRAMMAR *must, have to, should* (obligation)

**8** Complete the sentences with the correct form of *must, have to* or *should*. Use the information in brackets to help you.

1 Milo _____ write three ten-thousand-word essays for his course. (It's necessary)

2 We _____ tidy up the house. Jenna will be home soon. (It's a good idea)

3 You _____ park here. You'll get a fine. (obligation not to do this)

4 You _____ pay for children. They can come in for free. (It isn't necessary)

5 The sign says you _____ keep your dog on a lead. (It's necessary)

6 You _____ smoke anywhere in the building. It isn't allowed. (obligation not to do this)

7 You _____ wear a helmet when you ride your motorbike. It's the law. (It's necessary)

8 Do children _____ go to school on Saturdays? (Is it necessary?)

9 You _____ wear jeans to a job interview. (It isn't a good idea)

10 You _____ pay for the coffee. It's free. (It isn't necessary)

## VOCABULARY PLUS confusing words

**9** Complete the sentences with the words in the box.

| listen funny remember won hear |
| fun forgotten left |

1 I'm sorry. I can't _____ your name. Is it Sarah or Sue?

2 I think I've _____ how this machine works. Please show me again.

3 It's in my bag, which I've _____ in the car.

4 You never _____ to what I'm saying.

5 Sorry, the music's too loud. I can't _____ you.

6 I don't believe it. They've _____ the match.

7 I always laugh at his stories. He's so _____.

8 Why don't you come with us to the restaurant? It should be _____!

## GRAMMAR *used to, would*

**10A** Complete the text with *used to*, or *would* and the verbs in brackets. Where both *used to* and *would* are possible, use *would*.

FIVE YEARS AGO

Greg and Emily Bishop [1]_____ (live) on a small island in the Caribbean. They had a wonderful life. Greg [2]_____ (work) as a teacher in a local school, and Emily [3]_____ (study) for an online course at a university. They [4]_____ (have) a house on the beach, and after school, the children [5]_____ (play) on the beach with their friends. At the weekends, they all [6]_____ (enjoy) surfing, sitting on the beach, and eating delicious tropical fruit, like mangoes and pineapples. But when Greg's father became ill, the family decided to move back to the UK.

**B** Read about Greg and Emily's life now. Then complete sentences 1–6 with *used to* or *would*.

NOW

Greg runs his own taxi company, and Emily has a job working in a sports centre. The children don't enjoy school as much, and say they have to wear too many clothes all the time to keep warm. At the weekends, they all stay inside and watch football on television, and eat fish and chips.

1 Greg _____ (not have) his own business.

2 Emily _____ (not work) in a sports centre.

3 The children _____ (enjoy) school more in the Caribbean.

4 The children _____ (not wear) so many clothes to keep warm.

5 The family _____ (not stay) inside at weekends.

6 They _____ (eat) tropical fruit, not fish and chips.

## FUNCTION reaching agreement

**11A** Complete the phrases in the conversation with the words in the box.

| don't sure suggest need about What things that me |
| point agree should |

A: OK. As you all know, we had record sales last year, and we'd like to organise a celebration for all the staff. Any ideas for what we could do?

B: Well, I feel [1]_____ we should have a party here in the office.

A: That's OK by [2]_____.

C: I'm not sure that I [3]_____, actually. I think we [4]_____ think about going somewhere else. The way I see [5]_____, we spend every day in the office. Why [6]_____ we do something different to celebrate?

D: That's a good [7]_____. How [8]_____ if we go on a trip somewhere?

B: Yes. Or we could do a course together. There's a place where you can go and make chocolates, or bake bread or something like that.

D: I'm not [9]_____ that's a good idea. I [10]_____ we focus on things we all enjoy doing, like sport. [11]_____ about spending a day playing golf?

C: Golf! I don't think so.

A: OK. I think we [12]_____ to focus on whether we have a party of some kind, or go on a trip somewhere.

**B** Which phrases are used to give opinions? Which are responses to a suggestion or idea?

# TEST

**Circle the correct option to complete the sentences.**

1 Hi, Jake. What _____ this evening?

   a) you doing     b) are you doing  c) will you doing

2 I'm not sure. I think I _____ stay at home and study.

   a) will to        b) might      c) going to

3 We _____ Italy for our holidays. We love it there.

   a) are going to   b) will go      c) might going

4 We _____ about everything from politics to the weather. It's ridiculous.

   a) compliment   b) boast      c) argue

5 When Roberta comes round, we drink coffee and _____.

   a) apologise    b) chat       c) warn

6 He's changing his job in a month or _____.

   a) term        b) year       c) two

7 I think it will be better for everyone in the long _____.

   a) year        b) term      c) time

8 Look at the sunshine! You _____ have a great time at the beach.

   a) 're going to   b) 're likely to   c) may

9 We _____ never see him again.

   a) aren't likely to  b) may      c) won't

10 Yes, we're working against the _____ to finish in time.

   a) pressure    b) life      c) clock

11 Come on. Spill the _____. What did she say?

   a) peas        b) beans     c) tea

12 We don't know much about him. He's a dark _____.

   a) horse      b) dog      c) fish

13 She's been promoted and she's the top _____ now.

   a) fish        b) horse    c) dog

14 I'm sorry. I didn't _____ you were busy.

   a) recognise   b) remind    c) realise

15 I'm afraid I didn't _____ that. Can you say it again?

   a) catch      b) take      c) do

16 André is very _____. He wants to sell his designs all over the world.

   a) lazy        b) ambitious    c) indecisive

17 Françoise is a good _____. People really listen to what she has to say.

   a) risk taker    b) listener     c) communicator

18 The doctor said I _____ take these pills.

   a) has to      b) have to     c) haven't to

19 Help yourself to anything you want. You _____ ask.

   a) don't have to  b) have to     c) must.

20 It's a wonderful _____. I enjoy it a lot.

   a) work       b) study     c) job

21 I can't believe how big your kitchen is. It's _____.

   a) tiny        b) big       c) enormous

22 The interview was _____. I'll never get the job.

   a) brilliant     b) awful      c) exhausting

23 When I told my boss, he was _____.

   a) furious     b) terrible    c) impossible

24 As children, we _____ play at the bottom of the garden.

   a) used       b) use to    c) would

25 My mother _____ live in the mountains.

   a) used to     b) use to    c) would

26 If we work as a _____, we'll get the job done faster.

   a) boss       b) businessman  c) team

27 More than a hundred people had to _____ for a single job.

   a) compete    b) decide    c) get fired

28 The way I see _____, we need to start again.

   a) point      b) things    c) idea

29 That's OK _____ me.

   a) on        b) at       c) by

30 I think we need to sum _____ what we've learned.

   a) up        b) on      c) at

**TEST RESULT** | /30

## VOCABULARY technology

**1A** Underline the correct alternative.

1  He's six months old. He's been to the doctor to get his *genetic engineering / vaccinations*.

2  We are running out of coal, so the government is looking at new ways of making *electricity / computer networks*.

3  The government is planning to build new *nuclear power / genetic engineering* stations, but many people are worried that they are too dangerous.

4  The company has just invested thousands of dollars on its new *computer network / antibiotics* to improve communication between employees.

5  It sounds like you've got a chest infection. I think you need some *solar power / antibiotics*.

6  NASA has decided to restart its *communications satellites / space travel* programme and try to send people to Mars.

7  They rode their *commercial aeroplanes / motorbikes* right up through to the United States and Canada. The trip took several weeks.

**B** Match words in italics from Exercise 1A with definitions 1–8.

1  The science of changing the genes of a living thing _____

2  The energy created when you split or join two atoms _____

3  Drugs used to kill bacteria and cure infections _____

4  Power carried by wires and used to make lights and machines work _____

5  Exploration of the area beyond Earth where the stars and planets are _____

6  Machines that are sent into space and travel around the Earth, sending radio and television signals _____

7  Energy from the sun _____

8  An injection given to someone to protect them from a disease _____

**2A** Put the words in the correct column according to the pronunciation of the underlined letter *a*.

| space antibiotics nuclear travel machine |
|---|
| communications satellites vacuum |
| commercial aeroplanes solar vaccinations |

| /eɪ/  make | /æ/  apple | /ə/  polar |
|---|---|---|
| space | antibiotics | |

**B**  ▶ 5.1 Listen and check. Then listen and repeat.

## LISTENING

**3A**  ▶ 5.2 Listen to Mia, Tom and Owen answering the following questions. Write Mia (M), Tom (T) or Owen (O) next to the question they answer.

1  How has your country changed in the last thirty years? ___

2  Is the world getting better or worse? ___

3  How has your life changed in the last thirty years? ___

**B** Circle the correct option to complete the sentences.

1  Mia thinks that thirty years ago _____.
a) life was simpler
b) the pace of life was faster
c) people were happier

2  Mia thinks that email puts pressure on people because _____.
a) people's computers crash
b) emails sometimes don't arrive
c) we are expected to give an instant response

3  Tom says that Beijing has grown because people _____.
a) don't have as much money as before
b) came from around the world to get rich
c) came from all over China to make money

4  Tom says that life in the countryside _____.
a) has changed enormously because of the new technology
b) will never change because they do not have access to technology
c) has not changed that much, but people have more technology

5  Owen says that living conditions around the world _____.
a) are improving, even though many people are still living in terrible poverty
b) are terrible and are going in the wrong direction
c) are not improving, and more and more people are living in poverty

6  Owen thinks that there are _____.
a) fewer wars than before, but weapons are getting more dangerous
b) more wars than before, and weapons are getting more dangerous
c) the same number of wars as before, and weapons are getting safer

**C** Listen again and check.

## GRAMMAR comparatives/superlatives

**4  Complete the conversation with the correct form of the adjectives in brackets.**

A: I love my new digital camera. It was ¹_____ (expensive) my last one, but the pictures are much ²_____ (good) quality, and it's ³_____ (easy) to use.

B: But it's much ⁴_____ (big). Isn't it ⁵_____ (heavy) to carry around with you?

A: Actually, it was one of ⁶_____ (light) models in the shop. Although you can get ⁷_____ (small) and ⁸_____ (cheap) cameras, they're not as good as this one.

**5  Underline the correct alternatives.**

### WHAT'S YOUR FAVOURITE GADGET IN THE KITCHEN?

My favourite gadget in the kitchen is the dishwasher. It's ¹*much / a lot more* faster than me at washing up. The problem is that I'm getting ²*a slightly / a little bit* lazier.
*Yuri*

The toaster. Morning is ³*by far / slightly* the best time of the day for me. I enjoy a relaxing breakfast. And toast is ⁴*a lot / more* tastier than bread. I love it.      *Katia*

I don't cook very much, because I'm too busy. I have a microwave, which I find makes it ⁵*more / a bit* easier. Now, I eat ⁶*slightly / a little far* better than I did before.
*Nguyen*

## WRITING an essay; using discourse markers

**6A  Look at the task below and the notes a student has made. Tick the advantages and cross the disadvantages.**

**Discuss the advantages and disadvantages of studying English online, as opposed to in a classroom.**

1 flexibility – can study where and when you want, don't have to travel to a school

2 lack of interaction with your teacher or students

3 more choice – can choose to skip parts of the course, focus on other parts

4 IT problems – need to be confident with how the technology works, have good connections to the internet, etc.

5 discipline and time management – have to stay motivated

6 materials are technologically advanced – use a variety of multimedia materials

**B  Look at the two plans, A and B, for the essay. Which is better? Why?**

Many people now study English online. There are lots of good materials on the internet for doing this. As the technology increases, more and more people will try online learning.

But there are some problems, too. Online learning is boring because you are on your own. It's difficult to be motivated.

My opinion – I have tried online materials, and they are very good. But going to a class is a better way to improve your English.

[Plan A]

**Introduction:**
increase in technology means many people are now choosing to study English online, not in classrooms.

**Advantages:**
- increased flexibility
- increased choice of materials

**Disadvantages:**
- lack of interaction with teacher and students
- difficulty with motivation and discipline
- IT problems

**Conclusion:**
- Online courses offer students more choice and flexibility, but are more impersonal.
- Language is about communication, so face-to-face interaction with people in a classroom is a better way to learn.
- Online courses might be a good way to supplement your learning.

[Plan B]

**C  Look at the essay one student wrote. They forgot to use any discourse markers to link their ideas. Rewrite the essay, including discourse markers from the box where you see an asterisk (*).**

| One of the main advantages is that | However, (x2) |
| Another disadvantage is | In my opinion, |
| The problem is that | And another thing, |

With the increase in technology, many people are now choosing to study English online, rather than in the classroom. It's easy to see that there are many advantages to online courses. * There are also disadvantages.

* When you study online, you have increased flexibility to study when you want to, and where you want to. You have an increased choice of the materials you want to study, because you can choose them yourself.

* When you study online, there is a lack of interaction with your teacher and students. * You might find it difficult to stay motivated, and be disciplined with your studies. * You might experience computer problems, which make your study difficult.

* Online courses offer students more choice and flexibility. * They are more impersonal. As language is about communication, face-to-face interaction with people in a classroom is a better way to learn.

## VOCABULARY questions

**1** Cross out the alternative which is <u>not</u> possible in each sentence.

1 The class had a really good *debate / discussion / reply* about the environment.

2 In this study I will *investigate / wonder / discuss* the government's economic policy.

3 You should try to *respond to / enquire / reply to* emails as quickly as possible.

4 I *questioned / looked into / enquired about* renting a car, but it was too expensive.

5 A good *enquiry / question / wonder* always leads to more questions.

6 I've always *wondered about / questioned / responded* this man's motivation.

7 The *look into / research / investigation* was a waste of time; we found no solutions.

8 His newspaper column *debates / enquires / discusses* the issues of the day.

**2** Add the missing letters to complete the text.

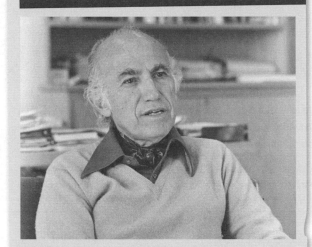

# WHO GOES FIRST?

Everyone involved in medical ¹re_search_ is eventually faced with a difficult ²qu_____: who will be my guinea pig? Who will be the first person to try this new medicine before we know if it works?

If we ³l_____ i_____ the history of drug testing, we find that many researchers not only ⁴de_____ this issue, but that a few have a surprising ⁵re_____: they use themselves as guinea pigs.

When scientist Jonas Salk was ⁶in_____ a new polio vaccine in the 1950s, he tried the drug on himself, his wife and children. It worked. Someone later ⁷en_____ about who held the patent (the right to sell the medicine). Salk's ⁸re_____ showed his character: he ⁹wo_____ why anyone wanted to make money from something that the world needed.

## GRAMMAR question tags

**3** Underline the correct alternative.

1 You're from France, *aren't you / weren't you*?

2 She broke a world record, *hasn't she / didn't she*?

3 They haven't seen us, *have they / haven't they*?

4 Don won't tell anybody, *does he / will he*?

5 That house looks nice, *isn't it / doesn't it*?

6 We didn't see that film, *did we / saw we*?

7 It hasn't rained for months, *has it / have it*?

8 You will come tomorrow, *won't you / will you*?

9 The shop doesn't open at 6a.m., *will it / does it*?

10 You stopped smoking last year, *didn't you / you didn't*?

**4** Read the situations and write questions. Use the correct question tags.

1 You think your friend is in love.
You <u>really like Mary, don't you</u>? (really like / Mary)

2 You leave the cinema laughing together.
That film _____? (be / funny)

3 Your friend's younger brother is going to borrow your car.
He _____? (not crash / the car)

4 You leave the football stadium after a boring match.
It _____? (not / be / very good / game)

5 You say goodbye to your friend at the airport.
You will _____? (write / to me)

6 You want to check that your friend got home safely last night.
You _____? (not miss / the last bus)

7 A tourist thinks you speak French.
You _____? (speak / French)

8 You have lost your watch.
You _____? (not see / my watch)

**5A** Read the conversations. Which responses are genuine questions (where Speaker B really doesn't know the answer)?

1 A: Have you met Yinka's parents?
  B: Only once. They're doctors, aren't they?

2 A: There isn't a cloud in the sky.
  B: I know. It's a beautiful day, isn't it?

3 A: Are you looking for the scissors?
  B: You haven't seen them, have you?

4 A: Have you read Jhumpa Lahiri's new book?
  B: Yeah, she's a great writer, isn't she?

5 A: I've got my final exam tomorrow.
  B: You'll pass, won't you?

6 A: I think this is the wrong address.
  B: Yes, we've made a mistake, haven't we?

**B** ▶ 5.3 Listen and check. Then listen again and repeat the responses. Use the same intonation in the question tags.

## READING

**6A** Read the introduction to the article. Which questions can you answer? Which can only be answered by experts?

### I never knew that!

What is worse for you: boredom or stress? Why is sea air good for you? If you throw water into the air during the Russian winter, will it come back down as ice? What three foods should you take to a desert island?

People love trivia*. In 2005, a book called *Does Anything Eat Wasps?* was a surprise hit. It was a collection of questions and answers from readers of a magazine called *New Scientist*. We at *Lynx Mag* decided to come up with our own questions and then we asked a panel of experts for answers.

*trivia: unimportant facts

**B** Read the rest of the text to find the answers.

**Q1: You are going to stay on a desert island for several months and you can only choose three foods to take with you. Which do you choose, and why?**
Broccoli, walnuts and orange juice. Broccoli has a chemical which helps detoxify your liver. It's also a superfood. Walnuts have protein and plenty of healthy fats. Orange juice is a source of clean water, and the orange contains Vitamin C. *Dr Leah Morecombe*

**Q2: What's worse for you: boredom or stress?**
Boredom. Stress can have benefits. Weight lifting is a type of stress. So are other sports and pressures at work. All of these are good for you in small doses. Boredom means you have no purpose in life, and no dose of boredom is good for you. *Dr Samran Naipaul*

**Q3: Why is sea air good for you?**
It isn't particularly. It got a reputation for being good for you in Victorian times because there was so much unhealthy smog in big cities. *Dr Robina Whitman*

**Q4: Why do flies like rotting food?**
Flies like rotting food because soft environments provide perfect conditions for breeding. When a fly's eggs hatch, the larvae live in and eat the rotting food until they grow into adult flies. *Dr Kelvin Marsh*

**Q5: If you throw water into the air during the Russian winter, will it come back down as ice?**
It depends where you are in Russia, and what the temperature is at the time. But, potentially, yes. At a temperature of -30°C, small amounts of water will turn into ice almost immediately. *Immanuel Kanevsky*

**C** Complete the questions for the answers.

1 Q: _____ helps detoxify your liver?
  A: Broccoli.

2 Q: What does the writer say _____?
  A: It can be good for you, while boredom can't.

3 Q: Who thought sea air was _____?
  A: The Victorians.

4 Q: What creatures live in and _____?
  A: Fly larvae.

5 Q: At -30°C, when will a small _____?
  A: Almost immediately.

**D** Find words in the text that match meanings 1–5.

1 remove dangerous chemicals or poison from something (paragraph 1) *detoxify*

2 measured amounts of something that you experience at one time (paragraph 2) _____

3 unhealthy air that is full of smoke and pollution (paragraph 3) _____

4 going bad; becoming soft and useless (paragraph 4) _____

5 when an egg breaks and a baby bird, fish or insect comes out (paragraph 4) _____

**VOCABULARY PLUS** word building: adjectives

**7** Complete the text with the correct form of the words in brackets.

### THE PNEUMATIC TYRE: HOW DID IT START?

John Dunlop, a Scottish vet, was [1]_____ (response) for one of the world's great inventions.

Dunlop's young son kept falling off his tricycle because the bumpy streets were [2]_____ (hope) for cycling. Dunlop thought of a [3]_____ (create) solution: filling the rubber tyres with air. This, he realised, would be an [4]_____ (ease) way to make the tricycle more stable.

He was right: it turned out to be a very [5]_____ (effect) solution. Lots of cyclists copied the idea and the air tyre became very [6]_____ (success). French car makers realised it was a [7]_____ (value) idea, and produced air-filled car tyres. The tyres also became very [8]_____ (profit); Dunlop Tyres is still a huge company today.

## VOCABULARY problems and solutions

**1** Complete the sentences with the words in the box.

> memory  switching  crashed  sort  work  print
> down  order  noise  recharging  fixing

1  I'm on the motorway, and my car's broken _____.

2  My phone isn't working. The batteries need _____.

3  We can't use the machines here because they're out of _____.

4  Can you call the maintenance department and tell them that the photocopier needs _____?

5  If it still doesn't work, try _____ it off and on again.

6  I don't believe it! My laptop's just _____ again!

7  Have you got another pen? This one doesn't _____ any more.

8  Don't worry about that now. I'll _____ it out later.

9  OK. First, you'd better save the documents onto a _____ stick.

10  I've got a copy on my computer. Do you want me to _____ you a copy?

## FUNCTION polite requests

**2A** ▶ 5.4 Listen to eight conversations. What does the person want each time? Match pictures A–H with conversations 1–8.

## B ▶ 5.4 Listen again. Complete the conversations with one word in each gap.

1  A: Excuse me, _____ you tell me the way to the swimming pool, please?

   B: Yes, of _____ I can. You keep going this way, until you get to the traffic lights. Then, …

2  A: Hello. Do you _____ what time the bank opens?

   B: I'm not _____. I'll just ask someone.

3  A: Do you want us to bring anything?

   B: That would be great. Could _____ bring some salad, and maybe something for dessert?

   A: Yes, _____ course. Anything else?

   B: No, that'll be fine.

4  A: Could you _____ me with my bags?

   B: I'm _____, I can't. I've got my hands full.

5  A: Would you mind _____ the door for me?

   B: Of course _____. There you are.

   A: Thank you. That's very kind.

6  A: Could you _____ me what time the show starts?

   B: _____ me have a look. The afternoon show starts at 3p.m.

   A: Thanks very much.

7  A: Would you _____ coming to get me from the station?

   B: OK. _____. Wait outside and I'll be there in ten minutes.

8  A: Do you know _____ there's a post office near here?

   B: Yes, _____ is – there's one just along this road.

## LEARN TO respond to requests

**3** Put the words in the correct order to make responses.

1  A: Would you mind saying that again?

   B: of / not / no, / course

   _____

2  A: Do you know how to get there?

   B: sure. / not / I'm / look. / me / have / a / let

   _____

3  A: Could you phone Tilly for me?

   B: course / yes, / of

   _____

4  A: Could you finish doing this for me?

   B: can't / I / afraid / I'm

   _____

5  A: Could you take these folders for me?

   B: I / yes, / can

   _____

## VOCABULARY  *-ing/-ed* adjectives

**1A**  Underline the correct alternative.

1  In three days we cycled 250 km. It was really *exhausted / exhausting*.

2  Everyone is very *worried / worrying* about losing their jobs.

3  I got stuck talking to a really *bored / boring* man.

4  I was *annoyed / annoying* because the class was cancelled again.

5  The car was travelling at a *frightened / frightening* speed.

6  I felt *embarrassed / embarrassing* about how untidy the house was.

7  He was totally *confused / confusing* by the tax form.

8  I'm going to have a nice, *relaxed / relaxing* bath.

9  I'm not really *satisfied / satisfying* with the way he cut my hair.

10  We were *shocked / shocking* when we saw the bill.

**B**  Find adjectives in Exercise 1A to match definitions 1–8.

1  not interesting _____

2  angry or irritated _____

3  very tiring _____

4  content, pleased _____

5  unclear or difficult to understand _____

6  uncomfortable and worried _____

7  upsetting and surprising _____

8  calming, helping you to rest _____

## READING

**2A**  You are going to read an article about why people get angry, and what happens. Before you read, number the events in the box according to categories 1–3 below.

1  Reasons    2  Consequences    3  Solutions

| |
|---|
| You start to shout. _2_ |
| You're irritated with someone. _1_ |
| You throw things around. _2_ |
| You do physical exercise. _3_ |
| You're frustrated about something. _1_ |
| You feel tense. _2_ |
| You try meditation. _3_ |
| People criticise you. _1_ |
| You distance yourself from the situation. _3_ |

**B**  Read the article and check.

# Stressed out?
## Take control.

We all know how it feels to get angry. Sometimes anger is mild, when you're just irritated with someone. But at other times anger can be more extreme, with explosive rages. You start to shout and throw things around. You lose control. Your blood pressure increases, your heart races, and you can't think about anything else. But what exactly *is* anger?

Anger is a normal response to a situation where you feel you are being attacked, treated unfairly, let down by others, hurt or rejected. Anger can help you to defend yourself, deal with the problem, and let others know how you feel. But anger can also cause problems. If you always lose control, people might start to avoid you. Friends and colleagues may be afraid of your temper, and leave you alone. Getting angry might make you feel better; giving you energy and making you feel like you're in control. But it might also leave you feeling hurt, and misunderstood. Also, getting angry doesn't usually solve the problem.

So, what can you do about your anger?

1  **Work out what makes you angry** – You need to understand what situations make you angry. Is it when people make comments about your work, or criticise you? Is it that you get angry when you're frustrated, and can't do the things you want? Do you get angry when you're tired? Understanding what makes you angry can help you to deal with the problem.

2  **Understand the signals** – Learn to identify the signs that you're getting angry. Do you start to shout and feel tense? Do you pace about the room? You need to recognise your own signs before you can change your behaviour.

3  **Take control of your mind and body** – Try taking a step back and distancing yourself from the situation, both physically and emotionally. Check your breathing, and take some deep breaths to slow you down, and calm your heart beat. Ask yourself, 'Am I overreacting?', 'Am I listening to what people are saying?' Can you find a way to be assertive, rather than aggressive? Try to speak calmly, rather than shout. Try the 'Is it worth it?' test. Ask yourself, 'Will it really matter in one month, one year?' Do some physical exercise, like going for a run or a swim. Or try some meditation, listen to music, or do whatever helps to calm you down.

**3**  Complete the statements with information from the article.

1  When you get angry, your blood pressure _____ and your heart speeds up.

2  Being angry about something can help others to _____ how you feel.

3  Getting angry is not usually a good way to _____ problems.

4  It's a good idea to understand what _____ make you angry.

5  If you recognise the signs that you are getting angry, then you can start to _____ your behaviour.

6  When you are angry, you should try to _____ yourself from the situation.

7  Deep _____ will help to calm your heart beat.

8  Try to speak _____ rather than shout.

## GRAMMAR zero and first conditionals

**4A** Complete the sentences with the correct form of the verb in brackets.

1 When Marianne _____ (find) a job, she _____ (leave) home.

2 Thomas _____ (get) a promotion if he _____ (work) harder.

3 If people _____ (exercise) regularly, they tend to _____ (live) longer.

4 If we _____ (leave) early enough, we _____ (miss) the traffic.

5 We _____ (start) the meeting as soon as everybody _____ (be) here.

6 If the music _____ (be) loud, people always _____ (dance).

7 When the weather _____ (be) good, we usually _____ (eat) outside.

8 If you _____ (use) sun cream, you _____ (not get) burned when we go sailing.

**B** For each sentence in Exercise 4A, decide if the situation is general (what normally happens – zero conditional), or specific (a possible situation in the future – first conditional).

1 *specific – first conditional*

2 _____

3 _____

4 _____

5 _____

6 _____

7 _____

8 _____

**5** Tick two correct sentences. Correct the wrong sentences.

1 If I find the book, I /^will^ send it to you.

2 If you will go to England, you will improve your English.

3 I'll tell him you called when I will see him.

4 If you give the plant too much water, it will die.

5 If they arrive early, will you to ask them to wait?

6 If you will come to the party tonight, will you bring a friend?

7 When I go to Krakow, I usually will see my aunt.

8 I always call my sister when there's a problem.

9 She will get angry if you will say that!

10 I go to the doctor tomorrow if I feel worse.

## VOCABULARY PLUS multi-word verbs

**6A** Circle the correct option to complete the sentences.

1 Don't forget to _____ when you've finished.
   a) click on    b) take off    c) log off

2 She's my best friend. We _____ really well.
   a) get off    b) get over    c) get on

3 I used to love Indie music, but then I _____ it.
   a) went off    b) got on    c) logged off

4 I _____ lots of different outfits, but I didn't like any of them.
   a) tried off    b) dressed up    c) tried on

5 Can you _____? I can't read what it says at the bottom of the screen.
   a) scroll on    b) scroll over    c) scroll down

6 You have to _____ your shoes when you go inside.
   a) log off    b) take off    c) dress down

7 He's nearly forty. It's about time he _____.
   a) settled down    b) went off    c) got on

8 I don't like going into bars on my own. I'm worried someone will try to _____.
   a) get on with me    b) chat me up    c) settle down with me

**B** Complete the multi-word verbs with a suitable particle.

1 I'd love to settle _____ and have children.

2 Unfortunately, I don't get _____ with his mother very well.

3 A very good-looking young man started to chat me _____ in the nightclub.

4 I think he went _____ me when he met my family!

5 Why don't you try _____ this shirt? I think it will really suit you.

6 Scroll _____ to the top of the page to find our contact details.

7 Do you mind if I take _____ my jacket? It's boiling in here.

8 Sorry, I didn't realise you needed the computer. I've just logged _____.

## VOCABULARY verb-noun collocations

**1** Complete the sentences with a verb from Box A and a noun from Box B.

A

watch   jump   hold   get   raise   do   cut

B

sale   queue   money   hair   experiments programme   seat

1 The scientists in our lab _____ a lot of _____ to find cures for common illnesses.

2 Did you _____ that _____ about UFOs on TV last night?

3 If you don't get to the show early, you won't _____ a _____.

4 The shop manager decided to _____ a _____ of last year's products.

5 Excuse me, you can't _____ the _____. Lots of people are waiting.

6 I asked my sister to _____ my _____ because I couldn't afford the hairdresser.

7 We're trying to _____ _____ for Save the Animals. Our target is €10,000.

## GRAMMAR second conditional

**2** Rewrite the sentences using the second conditional.

1 Joe goes to bed at 2a.m. He feels tired all the time.
  If Joe _didn't go to bed at 2a.m. he wouldn't feel tired all the time._

2 She doesn't play for the team – she isn't fast enough.
  If she _____.

3 We can't drive to your house because we don't have a car.
  We _____.

4 They won't pass the exam because they don't study.
  They _____.

5 I have a supportive family. My life is so easy.
  My life _____.

6 I'd love to buy that house, but I don't have the money.
  If I _____.

7 I'm so lazy. I don't write to my friends.
  I _____ lazy.

8 You don't water your plants regularly. They look so dry!
  If you _____.

9 Tom and Dave never help in the house. Their mother doesn't ask them.
  They _____.

10 I work on Saturdays. I can't come to the barbecue.
  If I _____.

**3** Put the verbs in brackets into the correct form. Use *would* or the past simple.

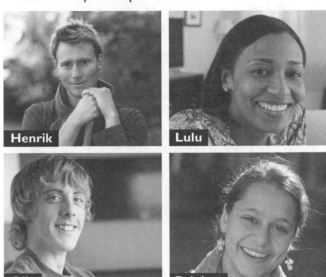

Henrik

Lulu

Olly

Brigitte

If you could choose any three things, what three things ¹_would make_____ (make) your life better? We asked this question to the public.

**Henrik, 25,** from Sweden, said, 'If I really ²_____ (have) a chance to change three things, they ³_____ (be) the environment, poverty and peace. My priority? I ⁴_____ (introduce) new laws to save the planet.'

**Lulu, 30,** from Edinburgh, had different ideas. She said, 'My life couldn't be better, but if I ⁵_____ (have to) change something, I ⁶_____(change) the colour of my curtains – they're a horrible grey!'

**Olly, 16,** from London, said, 'OK, if I ⁷_____ (be) able to change three things, first thing: I ⁸_____ (be) Prime Minister. Second thing: I ⁹_____ (make) rich people pay more tax. Third thing: I ¹⁰_____ (not let) people smoke cigarettes because they give you cancer.'

**Brigitte, 19,** from Germany, immediately said, 'More money! If I ¹¹_____ (be) richer, I ¹²_____ (not have) to work in this stupid shop! I could spend my days painting, which is my real dream!'

**4A** ▶ 6.1 Listen and write the sentences you hear. Write contractions as one word.

1 _____
  (9 words)

2 _____?
  (8 words)

3 _____
  (10 words)

4 _____
  (10 words)

5 _____?
  (9 words)

6 _____
  (8 words)

**B** Listen and repeat the sentences. Pay attention to the rhythm and the contractions.

## LISTENING

**5A**  6.2 Listen to the introduction to a radio programme. What is the topic?

**B** Look at the picture. Which people do you think are 'potential victims'? Why?

**C** ▶ 6.3 Listen to the rest of the programme and check.

**D** Listen again and complete the notes.

---

POTENTIAL VICTIM?

1 Woman with dog: <u>No</u>, because dogs are <u>unpredictable</u>.

2 Woman on mobile phone: _____, because she isn't _____.

3 Tourists looking at map: _____, because they are concentrating on the map, not _____.

4 Man leaving cashpoint: _____, because he didn't put the money _____.

5 Woman in mini-skirt: _____, because of her positive _____.

6 Big man in coat: _____, because he's looking at his feet and he doesn't know _____.

7 Couple leaving taxi: _____, because rule number one of the street is: if you have anything valuable, _____.

---

## WRITING  a letter of advice; qualifying what you say

**6A** Read the problem and choose the best summary.

a) Kathy doesn't want her friend to apply for a job because it is Kathy's 'dream job'.

b) Kathy's friend is angry because they both want to apply for the same job.

c) Kathy wants the same job as her friend, but she is worried their friendship will end if she gets it.

> Last week my colleague and best friend Mariela saw a job advertised in the paper. She told me it's her 'dream job' and she intends to apply for it. Unfortunately, it's also my dream job and I really want to apply. I have more experience than Mariela and would probably have a better chance of getting the job. But if I got it, it would ruin our friendship. Should I apply? And if I do, should I tell Mariela?
>
> *Kathy*

**B** Put the paragraphs in the correct order to make a letter of advice.

Paragraph 1: _____

Paragraph 2: _____

Paragraph 3: _____

Paragraph 4: _____

---

**???**

A How would you feel if you didn't apply, she did, she got the job, and you spent the rest of your career in the same job, bored and unhappy? Or how would you feel if, because of her getting this new job (which you *didn't* apply for), she lost daily contact with you, and your friendship broke up anyway? Wouldn't that be much worse than both of you applying and supporting each other?

B I know that close friendships can be ruined because one person becomes more successful than another. It happens all the time, and not only in Hollywood or on Wall Street. But this is no reason for you not to chase your dreams. Finally, here are a few questions for you.

C If she knows this, then that's the end of your problem. All you have to do is be honest with her and tell her that you want to apply. Then see what she says. If she is really angry, <u>perhaps</u> she isn't such a good friend. If I were you, I would also support *her* application as much as you can. Maybe offer to read through her CV and her application letter. If she gets an interview, give her a 'good luck' card and buy her a new pair of earrings to wear on the day. It's possible that neither of you will get the job, but tell her you'll be happy if either of you gets it.

D OK, so you work together and are best friends, too. This means that Mariela probably knows how you feel about your job and, in all likelihood, also knows your plans for your career. In all probability, she realises that this job is your dream job, too.

---

**C** Read paragraphs C and D again and underline six words/phrases for qualifying what you say. The first has been done for you.

**D** Read the problem. Write a letter of advice (180–200 words).

> In one month, an old friend of mine is getting married. He told me the date nearly a year ago. Unfortunately, I forgot this date and I have now booked a holiday with my new girlfriend on exactly the same day. I can't change the dates of the holiday because my girlfriend can only have this one week off. Her boss says she can't change the date. I really don't know what to do. Help!
>
> *Stefan*

## VOCABULARY life events

**1A Complete the sentences with the words in the box.**

> split  lost  pass  won  bought  accident  degree
> offered  place  promoted  engaged  failed

1  Did you _____ all your exams?
2  Sam had an _____ at work and had to go to hospital.
3  My boyfriend gets on so well with my boss, that he even _____ him a job!
4  Are you going to apply for a _____ at university?
5  Liz and Tony have been _____ for years, but they still aren't married.
6  Tom _____ his job at the factory.
7  I _____ my driving test six times!
8  My parents _____ up when I was three.
9  She _____ an international dance competition.
10 Helen got _____ to manager.
11 He's got a _____ in physics.
12 Last year they _____ a house on the beach in Brazil.

**B Match 1–6 with a)–f) to make phrases.**

1  pass        a) an accident
2  get         b) your job
3  win         c) with a partner
4  have        d) a competition
5  lose        e) promoted
6  split up     f) exams

## FUNCTION giving news

**2A ▶ 6.4 Listen and match conversations 1–8 with situations A–H.**

**B Cross out one unnecessary word in each sentence. Then listen again and check.**

1  Bad news, as I'm afraid.
2  I'm sorry for to have to tell you, but we lost the match.
3  I've got some good unfortunately news for you.
4  I'm afraid of I've got some bad news.
5  There's something who I've got to tell you.
6  You'll never guess what is happened.
7  It's unfortunately, we were burgled last night.
8  I've got something for to tell you.

## LEARN TO respond to news

**3 Complete the words in the responses.**

1  A: I've just passed my motorbike test!
   B: C_____! That's f_____ news.
2  A: Maciej's had an accident.
   B: That's t_____! I'm really s_____ to hear that.
3  A: I've just won the race!
   B: W_____ d_____. That's g_____ n_____.
4  A: He was attacked outside his house.
   B: That's a_____! Do they know who did it?
5  A: Amazing! I've just found €100 in an old coat pocket.
   B: H_____ you? You l_____ thing!
6  A: Unfortunately, he didn't get a place at university.
   B: That's a sh_____. I'm sorry to hear that.
7  A: I just bumped into Samantha on my way here.
   B: You're j_____! What's she doing here?

## VOCABULARY technology

**1  Add vowels to complete the words.**

1  I don't believe it. The __l__ctr__c__ty has gone off again.

2  He had to have a v__cc__n__t__ __n against measles.

3  I think sp__c__ tr__v__l is a complete waste of money.

4  I worry about g__n__t__c __ng__n__ __r__ng. I don't think we know enough about it.

5  We've put two huge s__l__r p__n__ls on the roof.

6  They're putting in a new c__mp__t__r n__tw__rk to improve communication.

7  N__cl__ __r p__w__r is dangerous because people make mistakes.

8  The region has much more tourism now that c__mm__rc__ __l __ __r__pl__n__s can fly here.

## GRAMMAR comparatives/superlatives

**2  Rewrite the second sentence so that it means the same as the first. Use the prompts in brackets.**

1  (slightly / warm)

The sea isn't as cold as it was yesterday.

The sea _____ than yesterday.

2  (far / expensive)

These black trainers are much cheaper than those white ones.

Those white trainers _____ these black ones.

3  (delicious)

I have never eaten a meal as good as that one.

That was _____ I've ever eaten.

4  (lot / easy)

I expected the exam to be more difficult.

The exam _____ I had expected.

5  (simple)

All the other solutions to the problem are more complicated.

It's _____ solution to the problem.

6  (much / happy)

I felt terrible yesterday, but today I feel much better.

I'm _____ today than I was yesterday.

7  (bit / short)

My brother is slightly taller than me.

I'm _____ my brother.

8  (bad)

Grandad thinks the world was a better place when he was young.

Grandad thinks the world is _____ it was when he was young.

## VOCABULARY questions

**3  Underline the correct alternative.**

1  I'd like to *discuss / inquire* this with my boss.

2  He didn't *answer / respond* to my email.

3  We need to *look / question* into the problem.

4  I'm *wondering / responding* if he'll take the job if we offer it to him.

5  I need to do some *research / debate* before buying a new computer.

6  The police are going to *wonder / investigate* the burglary.

7  We're getting a lot of *inquiries / question* about the new service.

8  It was a very interesting *debate / discuss* about immigration.

## GRAMMAR question tags

**4  Complete the questions with question tags.**

1  We can walk there, _____?

2  They've already left, _____?

3  We'll see you later, _____?

4  You don't like jazz, _____?

5  The film was great, _____?

6  You spoke to Mr Johnston earlier, _____?

7  You won't need the car, _____?

8  You haven't lost your keys again, _____?

## VOCABULARY PLUS word building adjectives

**5  Complete the words with the correct suffix.**

1  His shoulder is very pain_____. He says it hurts a lot when he tries to move it.

2  Unfortunately, the number of home_____ people living on the streets has increased.

3  I'm afraid I'm not respons_____ for what happened. It wasn't my fault.

4  He's one of Japan's most creat_____ film directors. His work is very original and exciting.

5  The situation seemed hope_____. What we were trying to do was impossible.

6  It's a very effect_____ way to teach reading – we've had excellent results.

7  Don't worry about the car, I'm just thank_____ that nobody was hurt.

8  She was always a mess_____ child. She just loved getting dirty!

## VOCABULARY problems and solutions

**6 Put the words in the correct order to make sentences.**

1 car's / down / the / broken

_____

2 phone / recharging / my / needs

_____

3 out / it's / order / of

_____

4 printer / fixing / the / needs

_____

5 it / switching / off / try / and / again / on

_____

6 this / it / strange / making / noise / keeps

_____

7 more / work / doesn't / any / it

_____

8 out / have / it / we / sort / to

_____

## FUNCTION polite requests; responding to requests

**7 Underline the correct alternatives.**

1 **A:** Could you *tell / to tell* me where I can find the manager?

  **B:** Yes, *of course / afraid.*

2 **A:** Do you know *if there's / if is there* a supermarket near here?

  **B:** I'm not *afraid / sure.*

3 **A:** Would you mind *checking / to check* the system for me?

  **B:** Of *course / sure* not.

4 **A:** Could you *see / to see* if anyone has arrived yet?

  **B:** Let me have a *look / course.*

## VOCABULARY -ing/-ed adjectives

**8 Complete the sentences with the correct form of the adjective in brackets.**

1 Are you _____ with me just because I'm a bit late? (annoy)

2 There's a _____ atmosphere in the school. (relax)

3 It's all very _____. I can't understand the results of this survey. (confuse)

4 She's _____ with doing the same thing every day. (bore)

5 I realised I'd made a terrible mistake. It was so _____! (embarrass)

6 I was still _____ from the race. (exhaust)

7 You look _____. What's wrong? (worry)

8 It was a very _____ experience. (frighten)

## GRAMMAR conditionals

**9A Underline the correct alternative.**

1 If I have time later, *I call / I'll call* you.

2 If I *don't / wouldn't* sleep well enough, I feel terrible the next day.

3 If there *is / would be* anything else you need, just tell me.

4 Those plants *die / will die* unless you water them soon.

5 If we had more room, *I'll / I'd* invite them to stay.

6 It wouldn't be as bad if we *didn't / don't* have so many exams this year.

7 If I didn't have a car, I *will / would* cycle everywhere.

8 If we *won't / don't* leave now, we'll be late.

9 It's more expensive if you *live / lived* in a bigger house.

10 If we *get / will get* hungry, we'll buy some sandwiches.

11 She *would / will* get angry if we asked her.

12 Life would be easier if we *will have / had* more money.

**B Circle the correct option to complete the sentences.**

1 If it rains tonight, _____.
  a) I take an umbrella
  b) I'll stay at home and watch a DVD
  c) I don't go out

2 If Justine passes her exams, _____.
  a) her mother is delighted
  b) she has worked hard
  c) she'll go to university

3 If you eat too much junk food, _____.
  a) it's not good for your health
  b) you would be too fat
  c) you'll like pizza a lot

4 If I had a garden, _____.
  a) I'd grow my own vegetables
  b) I sit in the sun all day long
  c) I'll grow lots of beautiful flowers

5 When I'm bored _____.
  a) I'd watch the TV
  b) always I cook something to eat
  c) I usually read a book

6 _____ at the cinema if you want.
  a) I'm meeting you
  b) I'll meet you
  c) I'd meet you

7 _____, I'll meet you later.
  a) If I get all my work finished on time
  b) If I'll finish work on time
  c) When I am finishing my work

8 He would look much better _____.
  a) when he'll buy some new clothes
  b) if he would sleep more
  c) if he cut his hair

## VOCABULARY PLUS multi-word verbs

**10** **Complete the sentences with *on*, *off*, *up* or *down*.**

1 I couldn't believe it when my brother's friend tried to chat me _____.

2 It was an informal family barbecue, so she dressed _____ in old jeans and a T-shirt.

3 You just need to click _____ the icon to open the file.

4 Can I try these jeans _____, please?

5 When you've finished on the computer, can you log _____?

6 She enjoys spending time with her dad, but she doesn't get _____ with her mum very well.

7 I was so embarrassed when he took _____ his shoes in the theatre!

8 I want to settle _____ and have children one day.

9 I used to drink a lot of coffee, but recently I've gone _____ it.

10 If you scroll _____, you'll find a link right at the bottom of the page.

## VOCABULARY verb-noun collocations

**11** **Circle the correct option to complete the sentences.**

1 They're _____ a plant sale in the village hall on Saturday.
   a) being          b) holding          c) doing

2 She's running a marathon to _____ money for cancer research.
   a) have           b) raise            c) do

3 They're _____ an experiment in bilingual education at my daughter's school.
   a) being          b) doing            c) having

4 If you get to the cinema early, can you _____ us some seats?
   a) have           b) put              c) get

5 Did you _____ that programme last night on killer whales?
   a) watch          b) seeing           c) look

6 How annoying. That man has just _____ the queue.
   a) held           b) walked           c) jumped

7 I think it's time I got my hair _____. It's far too long.
   a) wash           b) cut              c) dry

## VOCABULARY life events

**12** **Match 1–8 with a)–h) to make sentences.**

1 She didn't stop at a red light

2 The relationship wasn't working

3 I got a place at university

4 He did very well in the interview

5 They want to live together

6 She was brilliant at the job

7 He had an accident on holiday

8 He lost his job at the factory

a) so I'm going to study psychology.

b) so she got promoted.

c) so she failed her driving test.

d) so he's looking for work.

e) so they split up.

f) so he had to fly home.

g) so they offered him the job.

h) so they've bought a house.

## FUNCTION giving and responding to news

**13** **Find and correct ten mistakes in the conversations.**

**Conversation 1**

A: I'm sorry to have to telling you, but the train has been cancelled.

B: That annoying.

**Conversation 2**

A: I've got a good news for you.

B: What is it?

A: I've finished my painting.

B: Congratulation!

**Conversation 3**

A: There's something I've got to tell to you.

B: What?

A: I'm leaving San Francisco.

B: Oh. I'm sorry for hear that.

**Conversation 4**

A: You'll never guess to what.

B: What?

A: I got my promotion!

B: That's so fantastic news!

**Conversation 5**

A: Unfortunate, I didn't get the job.

B: That's real shame.

## TEST

**Circle the correct option to complete the sentences.**

1 Could you go and get the _____? I need to clean the floor.

  a) communications satellite  b) washing machine
  c) vacuum cleaner

2 Nowadays you can have a _____ to protect you from influenza.

  a) antibiotic  b) vaccination
  c) genetic engineering

3 Houses in the area have become much _____ recently.

  a) more affordable  b) more cheaper
  c) expensiver

4 People are able to work far _____ hours than before.

  a) most flexible  b) more flexible
  c) the more flexible

5 The saxophone is _____ to learn than some other instruments.

  a) slightly the hard  b) slightly easy
  c) slightly harder

6 That's a very good _____.

  a) wonder  b) inquire  c) question

7 I'm doing _____ into how computers affect children.

  a) a research  b) some research
  c) some investigate

8 You don't want to come with us, _____?

  a) would you  b) did you  c) do you

9 You've brought the camera with you, _____?

  a) did you  b) haven't you  c) didn't you

10 She _____ one of the best players in the world, isn't she?

  a) 's  b) will be  c) was

11 I couldn't do anything to make things better. I felt _____.

  a) effective  b) painful  c) useless

12 He's a very _____ puppy.

  a) lovable  b) creative  c) biological

13 My computer's _____. Can you help me?

  a) needs fixing  b) doesn't work
  c) crashed

14 Could you tell me _____?

  a) what is the problem  b) what the problem is
  c) what the problem

15 Sure. Let me _____.

  a) look for  b) have a look  c) look at

16 I've had a really _____ week.

  a) exhausted  b) tired  c) exhausting

17 I get really _____ when he doesn't reply to my texts.

  a) annoyed  b) annoying  c) boring

18 I'll give you the present when _____ you.

  a) I will see  b) I would see  c) I see

19 If we can arrange everything, _____ to France for a holiday.

  a) we'll go  b) we go  c) we would go

20 _____ very tired when I have to travel a lot.

  a) I'll get  b) I get  c) I would get

21 It's a formal evening, so we must _____ in something nice.

  a) dress down  b) dress for  c) dress up

22 We're very different characters, but we _____ well.

  a) get off  b) get on  c) get on with

23 She's selling the paintings to _____ for charity.

  a) buy money  b) earn money
  c) raise money

24 I'll get there early and get us some _____.

  a) seats  b) entrance  c) chair

25 If he _____ the drums late at night, I would sleep much better.

  a) doesn't play  b) didn't play  c) would play

26 Life _____ easier if we didn't have to work so hard.

  a) would be  b) is  c) was

27 I wouldn't mind if he _____ back again!

  a) always comes  b) never comes  c) never came

28 She was _____ a job at their head office in Washington.

  a) offered to  b) offered  c) promoted

29 I'm really pleased _____ you that you've won first prize.

  a) tell  b) to tell  c) telling

30 **A:** Their house burned down in a fire.

  **B:** Oh no. That's _____.

  a) a shame  b) annoying  c) awful

**TEST RESULT**    **/30**

## VOCABULARY success

**1** **Rewrite the second sentence so that it means the same as the first. Use the words in capitals and one other word.**

1 She was born with an ability to play the piano. NATURAL

She has a _natural talent_ for playing the piano.

2 He needs to concentrate on what he is doing. FOCUS

He needs to _____ what he is doing.

3 She put a lot of effort into her maths project. HARD

She worked _____ her maths project.

4 I want to improve my Russian, so I do it a lot every day. GET

I want to _____ at Russian, so I practise it every day.

5 He's someone who is very successful. ACHIEVER

He's a _____.

6 It's important to think that you have the ability to do what you want. BELIEVE

It's important to _____ yourself.

## READING

**2A** Write down three tips you would give to someone starting their own business.

**B** Read the text. Does it mention your ideas?

# MAKING IT HAPPEN

Women around the world setting up their own businesses may face similar kinds of barriers, despite the different contexts in which they live and work. But in spite of the problems they face, many have success stories to tell. We asked successful entrepreneurs for their tips for success.

### BRIDGING TWO CULTURES

When Jiao Lee moved to Ireland from China, she saw the opportunity to start a business which could help to build bridges between the two countries she loved. She started China Tours as a small travel business, setting up tours between the two countries. It was hard at first. She had to learn all about setting up a business in a foreign country, and she struggled with language barriers. But it was all worth it. China Tours now employs more than forty people, and has offices in Ireland and China. Jiao says, 'It has been such an exciting ride setting up China Tours, and I've enjoyed every minute. I wouldn't want to work for anyone else now.'

**Success Tip** – Always keep an eye open for an opportunity. And don't be put off when things seem hard in the beginning. Stick with your ideas, and soon you will find success.

### SWEET SUCCESS

When Carmen Spataro set up Sweet Dreams, a mobile cupcake business in her home city of Washington, she used social media to help spread the word about her new business. Travelling around the city in her pink van, selling her freshly-baked cupcakes, Carmen sends her followers updates on Facebook and Twitter, telling them where and when they can find the van. The idea has been a fantastic success, with customers sending each other messages about the new, delicious range of cakes on offer. 'I'm in cupcake heaven,' tweets one of her happy customers. 'I wasn't very confident with the technology at first,' says Carmen. 'But I learned quickly, and now I love it. Using social media has helped to add to the sense of fun which we wanted to establish.'

**Success Tip** – Keep up-to-date with technology, and use it to promote your business.

### HATS OFF

Melissa Faith had no idea that her designs for children's hats would lead her to success in business. She started by making a few hats to sell at a market. The hats were so popular that they sold out almost immediately. 'It was amazing. People were coming back for more, and I couldn't keep up with the demand,' she explains. Melissa set up a website to sell the hats online. Loopy Kids HatZone was an instant success, and Melissa now exports hats all over the world. 'One of the problems I've had,' says Melissa, 'is that I'm dyslexic, so it's hard for me to keep up with all the paperwork and emailing.' However, she thinks that her dyslexia also helps her to be more creative, and to have a fresh approach to problem-solving.

**Success Tip** – Be prepared for the unexpected. Some of the best things happen when you don't plan for them.

**3** Read the text again and mark the statements true (T), false (F) or don't know (DK).

1 Jiao Lee had previous experience in the travel industry.

2 She found that language was a problem in the beginning.

3 Carmen was confident with new technology.

4 She sells her cakes around the city from a mobile van.

5 Melissa had always planned to start a company selling hats.

6 She finds it difficult to be creative at work.

**4** Match words and phrases 1–6 from the text in Exercise 2 with definitions a)–f).

| | | | |
|---|---|---|---|
| 1 | barriers | a) | tell a lot of people about something |
| 2 | struggled with | | |
| 3 | (be) put off | b) | found it hard to do |
| 4 | spread the word | c) | make you not want to do something |
| 5 | keep up with | | |
| 6 | a fresh approach to (something) | d) | a new way of looking at something |
| | | e) | things that prevent you from doing something |
| | | f) | do something as quickly as you need to |

**GRAMMAR** present perfect simple versus continuous

**5** Complete the conversations with the present perfect simple or continuous form of the verbs in brackets. If both are possible, use the continuous form.

1 A: Your hair looks nice.

B: Thank you. I _____ (go) to a new hairdresser. It's much cheaper.

2 A: Do you know what time the package is being delivered? I _____ (wait) all morning.

B: I'll just check for you.

3 A: You look exhausted.

B: I know. I _____ (not sleep) well recently.

4 A: Are you OK?

B: Not really. The baby _____ (cry) all day. I don't know what to do.

5 A: Have you two met before?

B: Yes, we _____ (know) each other since university.

6 A: You look well. Have you been away?

B: Yes, we _____ (ski) in the Alps.

7 A: How long _____ they _____ (live) in Australia?

B: For about five years. They moved there to be closer to his family.

8 A: _____ you _____ (watch) that new detective series?

B: Yes, it's brilliant. I _____ really _____ (enjoy) it.

**6** Complete the email with the present perfect simple or continuous form of the verbs in the box. If both are possible, use the continuous form.

not decide   find   not have   think   happen   look
work (x2)   study   stay

Hi Nina,

How are you? Sorry I didn't write earlier, but so much ¹_____ in the last few weeks, I just ²_____ any spare time.

Luke and Shauna ³_____ with us. They were over from America, where Luke ⁴_____ on his new film. It was great to see them and catch up on their news. Apparently, they ⁵_____ about moving back to Asia, but they ⁶_____ for sure yet.

Things over here are good. We ⁷_____ for somewhere new to live. Our landlord wants us to leave, which is a shame. But we might ⁸_____ somewhere near the centre. It's a beautiful flat overlooking the river. And it's only five minutes' walk from the restaurant where I ⁹_____ at weekends. So, that would be fine. Jimmy ¹⁰_____ hard for his exams – they're next month, so keep your fingers crossed. I'll write again soon. Take care of yourself.

Much love,

Kelly

**VOCABULARY PLUS** verb phrases with prepositions

**7A** Match verb phrases 1–8 with a preposition from the box.

on   about   for   to

1 depend _____
2 succeed _____
3 pay attention _____
4 rely _____
5 pick up _____
6 have a talent _____
7 think _____
8 have access _____

**B** Complete the sentences with a suitable phrase from Exercise 7A.

1 You don't have to decide straightaway. Why don't you _____ it for a while?

2 This is important. Try to _____ what the man is saying.

3 Both solutions could be right. It _____ your point of view.

4 I'd like to _____ something you said earlier.

5 You obviously _____ music. You play very well for a beginner.

6 We _____ thousands of books in the university library.

7 I'm not sure if they'll _____ winning the election, but it's a good campaign.

8 I can't _____ you to be there on time, because you're usually late.

## VOCABULARY ability

**1A** Circle the correct options to complete the text.

Princess Diana

John Lennon

Schoolteachers may be experts ¹_____ their subjects, but they aren't always right about their students. Some of the most brilliant people in British history were ²_____ at school and got terrible reports. In his school report, John Lennon was described as '³_____ – certainly on the road to failure'. Winston Churchill, future Prime Minister and probably Britain's most ⁴_____ politician, clearly had a lot ⁵_____ as a student, but his behaviour was so bad that his teacher wrote, 'I really don't know what to do.' Stephen Fry's teacher didn't realise Fry had an ⁶_____ English. A fine actor, comedian and writer, Fry was bottom of his class. Robert Graves, a ⁷_____ schoolboy writer who became one of Britain's greatest poets, left school with this message from his headmaster, 'Well, goodbye, Graves and remember that your best friend is the wastepaper basket.' One of Diana, Princess of Wales's teachers was correct in that Diana wasn't a ⁸_____ student, but the teacher also wrote, interestingly, that she 'must try to be less emotional … with others.'

| | | | |
|---|---|---|---|
| 1 | a) at | b) for | c) in |
| 2 | a) useless | b) useful | c) gifted |
| 3 | a) skilful | b) hopeless | c) an expert |
| 4 | a) useless | b) hopeless | c) skilful |
| 5 | a) of ability | b) of skilful | c) of talented |
| 6 | a) expert in | b) aptitude for | c) aptitude to |
| 7 | a) gifted | b) expert | c) talent in |
| 8 | a) gifted at | b) expert | c) talented |

**B** Look at the words and phrases in the box and answer the questions.

> expert   gifted   have a lot of ability   have an aptitude for
> hopeless   skilful   talented   useless

1 Which two are negative? _____
2 Which two are adjectives that mean you are naturally very good at something? _____
3 Which is an adjective that means you are good at something (you practised it)? _____
4 Which is a noun that describes someone who knows a lot about something? _____
5 Which two phrases mean you are naturally good at something? _____

## GRAMMAR present and past ability

**2** Complete the text with the words in the box.

> manage   managed   to   was   wasn't   remember
> couldn't   could

### THE REAL RAIN MAN

A BARRY LEVINSON FILM
RAIN MAN

In 1989, actor Dustin Hoffman won an Oscar for his role in *Rain Man*. While accepting it, he said, 'My special thanks to Kim Peek for making *Rain Man* a reality.' But who was Kim Peek? Peek was a man with a mental disability, who ¹_____ do many simple things such as dressing himself, but could remember enormous amounts of information.

Peek didn't ²_____ to walk until he was four, but from the age of 16–20 months, he was able to ³_____ large amounts of information. As a teenager, he memorised whole books.

In later life, he ⁴_____ able to read a book in one hour and he remembered approximately 98.7 percent of everything he read. He ⁵_____ recite the content of around 12,000 books about history, geography, sports, and many other subjects. He was also able to ⁶_____ remember thousands of different pieces of music, though he ⁷_____ able to play them all because of his physical disability.

Kim travelled with his father all over the US and Canada, speaking about how he ⁸_____ to live a full life even though he was disabled. He died in 2009.

**3** Cross out the alternative which is **not** possible.

1 We *didn't manage to / couldn't / didn't manage* speak to John this morning.
2 I *can / am able to / do able to* speak five languages.
3 Ugo *managed to / could / was able to* finish the report yesterday.
4 Twenty years ago, I *was able to / can / could* run ten kilometres.
5 Few of us *can / are manage to / are able to* work without technology these days.
6 Women *didn't able to / weren't able to / couldn't* vote in Switzerland until 1971.
7 I *can't / 'm not able to / 'm not manage to* come to class tomorrow.
8 When we finished the work, we *were able to / could to / could* have a break.
9 *Are you able to / Do you can / Can you* use a computer?
10 *Did you manage / Were you able / Could you* to do your homework?

**4A** Read the pairs of sentences aloud. Tick the pairs that have the same number of syllables.

1 a) He's very gifted.
   b) She's really skilful.

2 a) He has an aptitude.
   b) I'm hopeless at this.

3 a) He thinks he's useless.
   b) She has a talent.

4 a) They say he's an expert.
   b) She has great ability.

**B** ▶ 7.1 Listen and shadow the sentences. Concentrate on the rhythm.

## LISTENING

**5A** Pictures A–F show moments in the life of a genius. What do you think is happening in each picture?

A seven months

B eighteen months — NEW YORK TIMES

C six years

D nine years

E DAILY NEWS Fall of a genius

F WILLIAM SIDIS 1898–1944

**B** ▶ 7.2 Listen to William Sidis's story and check your answers.

**C** Listen again and answer the questions.

1 Where were his parents from originally, and where did they move to?

2 What was William's first word?

3 How old was William when he could speak Russian, French, German and Hebrew?

4 What did he do at Harvard University when he was nine?

5 What did he do two years later?

6 Who 'followed him around'?

7 What two things did his sister say about his ability to learn languages?

8 For most of his adult life, what was Sidis 'running away' from?

## WRITING a summary; making notes

**6A** Read the notes for a summary of the story in Exercise 5. Then read audio script 7.2 on page 78 and answer the questions.

1 Find two mistakes in the notes.

2 Find two examples of places where the writer copied exact words.

### THE LIFE OF WILLIAM SIDIS

**Background**
- Lived in New York
- Father: psychologist at Harvard (Russian roots)

**Childhood**
- Born 1898
- 6 months: could speak. First word = 'moon'.
- 18 months: read newspaper
- 3 years: could type
- As a child, spoke Russian, French, German & Hebrew
- As a child, gave Maths lecture at Harvard Uni
- 11 yrs: attended Harvard Uni

**Adulthood**
- Wanted a quiet life
- Journalists followed him around and wrote articles about this young genius
- Didn't like fame
- 1944: died

**Myths**
- His sister = close 2 him & spoke about him after he died
- Knew all world's languages
- Took 1 week to learn a language
- IQ of 250–300

**Conclusion**
- Not all childhood geniuses will produce great things as adults
- Need to leave people alone to live their lives

**B** Which of the following are included in the notes? Tick the ones you find.

1 an abbreviation
2 a symbol for 'and'
3 a number to represent a word that sounds the same
4 a heading
5 a subheading
6 highlighted information

**C** Write a summary of the story (120–150 words) using the notes in Exercise 6A.

William Sidis is sometimes called 'the most intelligent man ever', but he isn't famous and his life was not full of great achievements. He was born ...

## VOCABULARY  qualifications

**1** What are the people in 1–10 talking about? Choose from the words in the box.

> qualifications    a certificate    a driving licence
> an online course    face-to-face learning
> distance learning    an apprenticeship    a degree
> an MA    a PhD

1  I got my first degree in 1990 and always wanted to study the subject more deeply so I finally began one last year. _____

2  I much prefer it because I like to be with other students in the same room. That's how I learn best. _____

3  My brother did one in a fashion company. They were nice to him and they showed him the basics of the business. _____

4  I don't really have any because I left school when I was fourteen, but I worked hard and was a success. _____

5  Mine is framed and hanging on my wall! It's evidence that I took the one-month course, and it was necessary for me to get a job. _____

6  When I finish school I'd like to go to university to study history, so I hope I'll have one by the time I'm twenty-one or twenty-two. _____

7  You really need it to be a university professor. It's the hardest academic qualification and it involves original research, but it's necessary. _____

8  I did one once. It was interesting because you write lots of messages to the other students but you never meet them. I passed. _____

9  It's the way education has been going for a long time. It means people from isolated parts of the world can study at a good university even if they can't travel there. _____

10  It took me five attempts to get mine! The first time I tried, I crashed and the instructor just said, 'OK, come back next week!' _____

## FUNCTION  clarifying opinions

**2A**  ▶ 7.3 Listen to conversations 1–3. What is happening in each one? Circle the correct option to complete the sentences.

**Conversation 1**

Parents are discussing a child's _____.

a) behaviour

b) TV-watching habits

c) school grades

**Conversation 2**

Colleagues are discussing _____.

a) another colleague's work

b) their qualifications

c) the best person for a job

**Conversation 3**

A presenter is asking a question about _____.

a) directing a play in a school theatre

b) the government's view of education

c) lack of money for the arts in schools

**B**  Listen again. Which sentence do you hear, a or b?

**Conversation 1**

1  a) In my view, it's getting out of control.
   b) For my view, it's getting out of control.

2  a) By example, she watched TV for six hours yesterday.
   b) For example, she watched TV for six hours yesterday.

3  a) I'm saying that's a lot.
   b) I must say that's a lot.

4  a) That's not what I'm saying. She's always in front of a screen.
   b) That's what I was saying. She's always in front of a screen.

**Conversation 2**

5  a) For me, Elizabeth is the best.
   b) To me, Elizabeth is the best.

6  a) For once, she has the right qualifications.
   b) For one thing, she has the right qualifications.

7  a) She would, but now I've said that, she already has a good job.
   b) She would, but having said that, she already has a good job.

**Conversation 3**

8  a) Yes, the reason I say this is that funding has been cut for arts subjects.
   b) Yes, it's reasonable to say that funding has been cut for arts subjects.

9  a) Let me give you an example. A school I visited last month wanted to do a play in the little school theatre.
   b) Let's look at the example. A school I visited last month wanted to do a play in the little school theatre.

10  a) I am thinking we could solve a lot of the problems if the government recognised the arts.
    b) I do think we could solve a lot of the problems if the government recognised the arts.

## VOCABULARY getting on

**1 Put the pairs of words in the box into the correct places in sentences 1–10 below.**

> on my    us over    ~~on well~~    disturb me
> friends    with    a nuisance    ask a
> my own    to know    to myself

1 Joachim gets ∧*on well* with his mother, but he's always arguing with his father.

2 Can I favour? Would you mind opening the window for me?

3 Whenever they're arguing, I prefer to mind business. I don't get involved.

4 Hayley has invited for dinner at her house. Can we go?

5 Those neighbours are – they're always playing loud music and making a mess.

6 She got her neighbours immediately. They were really friendly and chatty.

7 Please don't. I'm trying to do some work.

8 One thing that gets nerves is when the neighbours have noisy parties!

9 Xun hasn't made her neighbours yet, but she only moved in last week.

10 I keep myself. I hate chatting about nothing – it's a waste of time.

## GRAMMAR articles and quantifiers

**2 Add *a*, *an* or *the* where necessary.**

1 Do you want ∧*a* drink?

2 Have you received letter I sent you?

3 Dogs are wonderful pets.

4 Do you have pen I can borrow?

5 She went to Paris on Wednesday.

6 Is there airport in the city?

7 I'm going to Germany in morning.

8 We live by Pacific Ocean.

9 My brother is actor.

10 Nurses aren't paid enough.

11 He doesn't have children.

12 Did you see film I told you about?

13 I live in United States.

14 She's nicest woman I know.

15 Do you like apples?

**3 Make sentences with one word or phrase from each section.**

| | | |
|---|---|---|
| 1 ~~We went there for a~~ | a) of us love this | i) of friends in this community. |
| 2 There are plenty | b) of good restaurants in the town, | ii) in Poland when I was younger. |
| 3 I don't know | c) many cars in most | iii) I like the architecture. |
| 4 All | ~~d) few days in~~ | iv) ~~June last year.~~ |
| 5 If you have enough | e) lots | v) place because it's so friendly. |
| 6 There are too | f) much about this city, but | vi) especially if you like French food. |
| 7 I've got | g) time, go | vii) to the museum – it's great. |
| 8 I spent a bit | h) of time | viii) big cities – I hate traffic! |

1 *We went there for a few days in June last year.*

2 _____

3 _____

4 _____

5 _____

6 _____

7 _____

8 _____

**4 Read the text. Which lines are correct? Which have an extra word?**

| | |
|---|---|
| In the past, a small English village called ~~the~~ Lanreath, in Cornwall, | 1 *the* |
| had three pubs, two shops, and a post office. Now it doesn't have | 2 ✓ |
| but any of these. The post office, the last shop and the last pub | 3 ___ |
| were all of recently closed down. Now the council wants | 4 ___ |
| to close the primary school. The school has had excellent | 5 ___ |
| results and is very popular with children and parents. The | 6 ___ |
| problem is that the school doesn't have enough students, and | 7 ___ |
| the council says it costs too much to money to keep it open for | 8 ___ |
| only a small few children. The villagers decided to fight the | 9 ___ |
| council's ruling. The whole village packed up, including sheep and | 10 ___ |
| cows, and travelled a five hours to London. They went to a | 11 ___ |
| park and created a miniature Lanreath. They showed the more | 12 ___ |
| best of village life, playing traditional games, doing a traditional | 13 ___ |
| dance, and holding a cake sale. Some of all the teachers also taught | 14 ___ |
| a lesson for Lanreath Primary School pupils. | 15 ___ |
| The BBC made a TV programme about the story: *Power To The* | 16 ___ |
| *People: The Invasion of Islington*, presented by a Tim Samuels. | 17 ___ |

## LISTENING

**5A** ▶ 8.1 Listen to interviews with Elise and Marc about neighbours and answer the questions for each person.

1 Who are their neighbours?

Elise: _____

Marc: _____

2 Why do they like the situation with their neighbours?

Elise: _____

Marc: _____

3 How often do they see their neighbours?

Elise: _____

Marc: _____

4 How long have the people lived there?

Elise: _____

Marc: _____

**B** Complete the summaries with one word in each space. Then listen again and check.

Elise says she has the ¹_____ neighbours. She sees them a lot because she works in the ²_____ business. Her extended family consists of ³_____ people. They eat together every ⁴_____. She thinks this situation is ⁵_____ in many countries. She has never asked her ⁶_____ if he likes living so close to her family.

Marc's nearest neighbours are two cows that live ⁷_____ miles away! Marc and his wife used to live in ⁸_____, but they didn't like the crowds, the noise and using public ⁹_____. They bought a ¹⁰_____ ten years ago. Marc and his wife work ¹¹_____. Marc says the interviewer is the ¹²_____ person they've seen this year!

**C** Circle the best alternative way of saying these extracts from the interviews.

1 if I need a babysitter for my kids …

 a) if I need someone to look after my children …

 b) if my children need to sit still …

2 You never get fed up with the family?

 a) You never eat with the family?

 b) You never get tired of the family?

3 We always wanted to live side by side.

 a) We always wanted to live in the same town.

 b) We always wanted to live next to each other.

4 We really are completely isolated.

 a) We really like to be close to nature.

 b) There are no other people near us.

5 It's not a functioning farm.

 a) The farm doesn't make much money.

 b) The place isn't actually used as a farm.

6 We're a bit antisocial.

 a) We don't like mixing with other people.

 b) We don't like working for big companies.

## VOCABULARY PLUS compound nouns

**6A** Match the words in box A with the words in box B to make compound nouns.

A

| | | | | | |
|---|---|---|---|---|---|
| ~~traffic~~ | high | housing | sports | industrial | car super |

language shopping one-way terraced outdoor gift primary

B

houses ~~lights~~ shop school (×2) centre (×2) street (×2) park market (×2) estate (×2)

1 *traffic lights* _____    8 _____

2 _____    9 _____

3 _____    10 _____

4 _____    11 _____

5 _____    12 _____

6 _____    13 _____

7 _____    14 _____

**B** ▶ 8.2 Listen and check. Then listen and repeat. Concentrate on the stress patterns.

**7** Complete the sentences with a compound noun from Exercise 6A.

1 My best friend lives in a house on a big new _____ in Bristol.

2 I'm studying English for six weeks in a _____ in Bath.

3 My son will be old enough to go to _____ next year.

4 You can't drive your car down there – it's a _____!

5 I use the gym in the _____.

6 We live in a row of small _____ in Barton Road.

7 Drive along the High Street and turn left at the _____.

8 We left the car in the _____ while we went shopping.

9 I buy my food in the _____ because it's more convenient than going to lots of small shops.

10 There's a _____ in the art gallery where you can buy postcards of some of the paintings.

11 Our town has an _____ every Thursday behind the bus station – I buy all my vegetables there.

12 Ben's new company has an office on an _____ just outside Coventry.

13 There's an internet café in the _____, between the cinema and the book shop.

14 My daughter and her friends spend most Saturdays in the _____, although I don't think they buy much!

## VOCABULARY the internet

**1  Read the situations and write the type of website or web page a)–l) the speakers need.**

1  'I want to write my day-to-day thoughts and publish them on the internet.' _Blog_____

2  'I need my own website that tells people who I am and what I do.' _____

3  'I just need to find some information very quickly.'

4  'I'm looking for love.' _____

5  'I want to put my photos on the net so my friends and family can see them.' _____

6  'I need some information about a big company that I might work for.' _____

7  'I want to find out what's going on in the world.'

8  'I want to make new friends and find out what my old friends are doing.' _____

9  'I want to find out the best places to go for a holiday.'

10  'I'd like to read short reviews of films, restaurants, etc., to see which are the best.' _____

11  'I'd like to see this film clip that my friend uploaded onto the net.' _____

12  'I want to write an online encyclopedia that everyone can contribute to.' _____

a) blog
b) photo sharing site
c) ratings site
d) video sharing site
e) social networking site
f) search engine
g) wiki
h) travel site
i) news site
j) personal homepage
k) dating site
l) corporate website

## GRAMMAR relative clauses

**2  Match each pair of sentences with the correct explanation, a) or b).**

1  The children, who love films, went to the cinema.   *b*

2  The children who love films went to the cinema.   *a*

   a) Only some of the children went to the cinema.

   b) All of the children went to the cinema.

3  Her brother, who is a musician, lives in New York.

4  Her brother who is a musician lives in New York.

   a) She has one brother. He lives in New York.

   b) She has more than one brother. One of them lives in New York.

5  My house, which is by the beach, has a great view.

6  My house which is by the beach has a great view.

   a) I have more than one house.

   b) I have only one house.

7  They went to the only school in the village, which had good teachers.

8  They went to the only school in the village which had good teachers.

   a) There was more than one school in the village, but only one had good teachers.

   b) There was only one school in the village.

**3  Complete the quotations of definitions with the words in the box.**

> thing that   who behaves   clothing that   which has
> person who   place where   name that   a place

1  'A jumper is an item of _____ _____ is worn by a child when his or her mother is cold.'

2  'A dictionary is the only _____ _____ success comes before work.'

3  'A coward is a _____ _____, when faced with danger, thinks with his feet.'

4  'Experience is the _____ _____ men give to their mistakes.'

5  'A cigarette is a bit of tobacco in paper _____ _____ fire at one end and an idiot at the other.'

6  'An advertisement is a _____ _____ persuades you to spend money you don't have on things you don't need.'

7  'A babysitter is a teenager _____ _____ like an adult so adults can behave like teenagers.'

8  'A bank is _____ _____ where you keep the government's money in your name.'

**4  ▶ 8.3 Listen for the pauses where there are commas. Tick the sentence you hear.**

1  a) The website which we built is too slow.

   b) The website, which we built, is too slow.

2  a) Those people who are always working don't enjoy life.

   b) Those people, who are always working, don't enjoy life.

3  a) The ratings site which I check every day is growing fast.

   b) The ratings site, which I check every day, is growing fast.

4  a) Those students who do online courses love studying.

   b) Those students, who do online courses, love studying.

5  a) Near my flat where you're staying there's a supermarket.

   b) Near my flat, where you're staying, there's a supermarket.

# COUCHSURFERS – THE COMMUNITY THAT WON'T LIE DOWN

1 One April, Casey Fenton bought a cheap ticket from the United States to Iceland. He planned to stay for a long weekend. There was just one problem: he had nowhere to sleep. He didn't want to stay in a hotel, so he emailed 1,500
5 students in Reykjavik, Iceland's capital, asking if he could sleep on someone's couch. Amazingly, he had dozens of replies. After a wonderful weekend with his new friends, he realised that there was a fantastic opportunity for cultural exchange through 'CouchSurfing'. He decided to start a website to make
10 CouchSurfing possible.

2 www.CouchSurfing.org was launched in 2003. Its mission statement said that the idea was to 'create inspiring experiences', with a focus on cross-cultural sharing. Since then, tens of thousands of people have stayed on strangers' couches
15 in 230 countries, had the chance to see places through the eyes of a local person, and made wonderful friendships.

3 So how does it work? If you want to be a host, you write your profile on the website, saying where you live, your age, job and hobbies. If you want somewhere to stay, you type the
20 name of the city. A list of people appears. You look at their profiles and photos and choose a person. Then you contact them to see if they are free. In many cases, they meet you for a coffee first before allowing you into their home. Then, if you seem normal and friendly, they let you stay on their couch.

25 4 The idea of CouchSurfing seems dangerous. Would you really want to stay with a stranger? The website has several ways to protect its users. Before choosing a person to stay with, you can read what other CouchSurfers say about them. There is also a system of 'vouching'. This means that other people
30 promise that your host has a good character. It is impossible to make CouchSurfing completely safe, but there have been no horror stories so far.

5 And the benefits? Here's what the CouchSurfers say on the website. 'It offers me a window to see the beautiful planet in
35 the best way.' (Liu, China); 'What a great way to travel and meet people!' (Cecilia, Paraguay); 'CouchSurfing changed my life. Meeting people all around the world, discovering
40 their way of life, their culture, getting new friends, … everything become possible with CouchSurfing.'
45 (Kim, Malaysia)

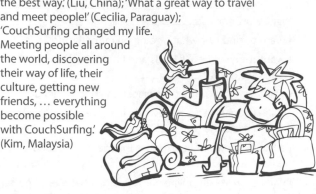

## READING

**5A** Look at the picture and the title of the text. What do you think a *CouchSurfer* is?

**B** Read the text and answer the questions.

1 What problem did Casey Fenton have concerning his trip to Iceland? _____

2 Who did Fenton write to, and what happened next?

_____

3 What does the website say CouchSurfing focuses on?

_____

4 What are the four stages for finding someone to stay with?

_____

5 How does the website try to make CouchSurfing safe?

_____

**C** Match words 1–5 from the text with definitions a)–e).

1 a dozen (paragraph 1)
2 to launch (paragraph 2)
3 a mission statement (paragraph 2)
4 inspiring (paragraph 2)
5 a profile (paragraph 3)

a) so good or successful that it makes people want to do something
b) a text that explains the purpose of an organisation
c) to start something big or important or make a new product available
d) a short description that gives the main details of what someone is like
e) twelve

## WRITING a website review; using complex sentences

**6A** Complete gaps 1–4 in paragraphs A–D with the words in the box.

like   feature   best   would

A ☐ Another ¹_____ I like is the book reviews. Regular users of the website often write these. Even though the writers aren't professionals, some of the reviews are excellent, and they give you a good idea of what's in the book.

B ☐ One website I really ²_____ is amazon.com. It is a website for buying books. One reason I'd recommend it is because you can buy used books. This means you can get really good books for half the price they cost in the shops.

C ☐ Finally, I ³_____ recommend this website to anybody who is interested in books. Even if you don't buy anything, it is fun to surf the site, and a great source of information about books of all types.

D ☐ The ⁴_____ thing about Amazon, though, is the fact that it is so easy to use, and you can trust it. I have ordered dozens of books through Amazon, and the books have always arrived quickly and in good condition.

**B** Put the paragraphs of the website review in the correct order.

**C** Write a website review (120–150 words).

## VOCABULARY welcoming

**1A** Make phrases for welcoming with the words in the boxes. Then complete the conversations.

> at    mess    make    the    yourself    help    home    excuse    yourself

1 A: Can I try one of these cakes?

   B: Yes, _____.

2 A: Come in. _____.

   B: It looks very tidy to me. You should see my place!

3 A: Welcome! _____.

   B: Thanks. What a nice room.

> my    seat    up    guest    put    a    be    your    have    feet

4 A: May I use your phone, please?

   B: _____.

5 A: Good morning. I'm here to see Mr Drucker.

   B: I'll tell him you're here. _____.

6 A: You must be exhausted. _____.

   B: Thank you. Yes, it was a really tiring day.

**B** Match pictures A–F with the conversations in Exercise 1A.

## FUNCTION being a good guest

**2** Tick the correct sentences.

1 a) Is it OK if I arrive half an hour late?

   b) Is it OK if I am arrive half an hour late?

2 a) What we should do if we get lost?

   b) What should we do if we get lost?

3 a) Do I need to bring a present?

   b) Do I need bring a present?

4 a) Was I did something wrong?

   b) Did I do something wrong?

5 a) Is this a bad time? I come back later.

   b) Is this a bad time? I can come back later.

6 a) If I'm you, I'd apologise.

   b) If I were you, I'd apologise.

7 a) Sorry about that. I didn't know.

   b) Sorry for that. I didn't know.

8 a) My apologise. I didn't realise.

   b) My apologies. I didn't realise.

9 a) No, it's not the necessary.

   b) No, it's not necessary.

10 a) Don't worry. It's fine.

   b) You don't worry. It's fine.

## LEARN TO accept apologies

**3** Underline the correct alternative.

1 A: I'm really sorry. I broke this cup.

   B: *It's no problem. / It's not the problem.*

2 A: Sorry, I didn't phone you before coming. I can see you're busy.

   B: *Not at all. / Not all.* I'll be finished in just a minute.

3 A: My apologies. I didn't realise you were working.

   B: *That's too right. / That's all right.* I'm not doing anything important.

4 A: Sorry, did I do something wrong? I didn't know I had to shake everyone's hand.

   B: *It's very fine. / It's fine.* I don't think anyone noticed.

5 A: I forgot to send you the notes from the last meeting. Sorry about that.

   B: *Nothing. / It's nothing.* Don't worry about it.

6 A: I'm sorry. I didn't bring anything for the children.

   B: *You really don't have to. / You really haven't to.* They're just happy to see you.

7 A: I'm sorry. I didn't realise I had to print the tickets out.

   B: Don't worry. *We can sort it out. / We can sort out it.*

## VOCABULARY success

**1** Tick two correct sentences. Correct the wrong sentences.

1 Our company focuses at quality software.
2 She's getting better at maths.
3 It's important that we work hardly at this.
4 The key is to believe of yourself.
5 He is certainly a high achiever.
6 We'll improve if we are practise every day.

## GRAMMAR present perfect simple versus continuous

**2** Underline the correct alternative.

1 How long have you *known / been knowing* David?
2 She's angry – she's *waited / been waiting* for an hour!
3 This morning I've *read / been reading* a book called *Infinite Jest* – it's over a thousand pages long!
4 How many people have you *invited / been inviting* for this party?
5 My hands are dirty, I've *worked / been working* on the car.
6 For the last six years I've *learned / been learning* Arabic, but it's really difficult.
7 They don't want to rent *The Godfather* because they've *seen / been seeing* it already.
8 Hello. I don't think we've *met / been meeting* before.

## VOCABULARY PLUS verb phrases with prepositions

**3** Complete the text with the correct prepositions.

### TOP BLOGGERS

The best bloggers pay attention [1]_____ what's going on in the world. They listen [2]_____ influential people, pick up [3]_____ the stories in the air and put [4]_____ hours reading websites and doing their research. They don't just wait [5]_____ the big stories; they find them in the corners where other people aren't looking. Of course, they rely [6]_____ traditional media such as newspapers. All bloggers depend [7]_____ other sources for their content, but they think [8]_____ the issues and, rather than just agreeing [9]_____ the journalists, they look [10]_____ alternative opinions. Often the best bloggers belong [11]_____ groups or societies that have access [12]_____ interesting people, so the bloggers can hear different opinions. The most important qualities for someone to succeed [13]_____ the 'blogosphere' are to have a talent [14]_____ writing and to believe [15]_____ yourself. In this sense, they have a lot in common [16]_____ traditional journalists, but bloggers don't have to worry [17]_____ newspaper deadlines. The negative side? Bloggers usually don't get paid [18]_____ their work.

## VOCABULARY ability

**4** Put the words in the correct order to make answers to the questions.

1 A: Why do you think they asked him to write the textbook?
 B: subject / because / expert / he's / his / an / in
 _____

2 A: Why do you think he'll pass the exam?
 B: of / he / maths / because / lot / ability / has / in / a
 _____

3 A: Why do you think she'll become an Olympic gymnast?
 B: sport / she's / the / at / gifted / because
 _____

4 A: Why do you think they'll do well in Hollywood?
 B: talent / have / writing / because / a / scripts / for / they
 _____

5 A: Why do you think he'll become a professional golfer?
 B: aptitude / the / has / an / because / game / for / he
 _____

6 A: Why do you think you'll fail the test?
 B: science / at / absolutely / because / hopeless / I'm
 _____

## GRAMMAR present and past ability

**5** Rewrite the second sentence so that it means the same as the first. Use the words in capitals. Write three words. Contractions are one word.

1 We don't know how to play cards. CAN'T
 _____ cards.

2 She is a wonderful singer. CAN
 _____ really well.

3 Can you bring some drinks to the party? ABLE
 _____ to bring some drinks to the party?

4 We didn't have time to visit Las Vegas. MANAGE
 We _____ visit Las Vegas.

5 I failed the test. ABLE
 I _____ pass the test.

6 I can usually clean the house in about two hours. MANAGE
 I usually _____ the house in about two hours.

7 What languages were you able to speak when you were a child? COULD
 What languages _____ when you were a child?

8 They succeeded in breaking the record. MANAGED
 They _____ the record.

## VOCABULARY qualifications

**6** Complete the text with the words in the box.

> Master's   apprenticeship   licence   distance
> qualifications   online   degree   learning

**YOUTH WORK**

When I left school, I had no ¹_____ except my driving ²_____. I needed that because I spent most of my time in stolen cars. When I was eighteen, a friend of my father's told me I could do an ³_____ in his printing company, but because I couldn't read or write, I refused. Instead, I got involved in serious crime. Aged nineteen, I was sent to prison. This was my first taste of real education. Although there was no formal face-to-face ⁴_____, one of the inmates taught me to read and write. Later, he told me about ⁵_____ learning. We were allowed access to computers for a few hours a week, so I started an ⁶_____ course. After three years, I got a ⁷_____ in psychology. It was the best day of my life. When I left prison, I went on to do a ⁸_____, and I became a youth worker, advising young people how to avoid a life of crime.

## FUNCTION clarifying opinions

**7A** Underline the correct alternatives.

A: In my ¹*views / view*, sport is wonderful. The ²*reasoning / reason* I say this is that it makes people work in teams. ³*For / To* me, it's really important.

B: I ⁴*can / must* say I agree with you. ⁵*And / For* one thing, it keeps you healthy. For ⁶*another / other*, it's good for your character. ⁷*For / In* example, you learn teamwork.

A: That's ⁸*it / what* I was saying: you learn to work together And like I ⁹*told / said*, it's also good for your health.

B: That's right. I ¹⁰*will / do* think children should play more sport in school.

A: And they can join clubs, too. Let me ¹¹*do / give* you an example: my kids are in an after-school athletics club.

B: That's great. Having ¹²*said / spoken* that, those clubs can be very expensive.

**B** Which of the expressions 1–12 in Exercise 7A are for giving opinions (O)? Which are for giving examples (E)? Which are for referring to what you said earlier (R)?

| | |
|---|---|
| 1 _____ | 7 _____ |
| 2 _____ | 8 _____ |
| 3 _____ | 9 _____ |
| 4 _____ | 10 _____ |
| 5 _____ | 11 _____ |
| 6 _____ | 12 _____ |

## VOCABULARY getting on

**8** Put the letters in brackets in the correct order to make a word. Then rewrite the sentences using that word and <u>two</u> other words.

1 That music is really annoying. (revesn)
   That music really gets *on my nerves*_____.

2 I don't like mixing with other people. (mlseyf)
   I prefer to keep _____.

3 She's always helping me. (frvouas)
   She's always _____.

4 Why don't you stop interfering in my life? (binesssu)
   Why don't you mind _____?

5 They asked us to have dinner with them. (orev)
   They invited us _____.

6 I have a great relationship with my dad. (lwle)
   My dad and I _____.

## GRAMMAR articles and quantifiers

**9** Are the two underlined parts of the sentences correct? Change the ones that are wrong.

1 I went to school in a <u>small town</u> in ✓ *the* <u>United States</u>.

2 My cousin, who is from <u>the West Indies</u>, is <u>an architect</u>.

3 <u>Golf players</u> don't usually make much money, but <u>best ones</u> are millionaires.

4 We saw <u>a rat</u>. The next day our cat killed <u>rat</u>.

5 I didn't enjoy a party – there were <u>too much people</u>.

6 Do you know <u>any good hairdressers?</u> I need <u>the haircut</u>.

7 <u>Plenty of people</u> would happily pay to travel to <u>Moon</u>.

8 I need an MA, but it takes <u>too many time</u> and I don't have <u>enough money</u>.

9 To finish the dish, add a <u>little salt</u> and <u>lot of pepper</u>.

10 <u>Some of us</u> are planning to go to <u>the Barcelona</u> this weekend.

## VOCABULARY PLUS compound nouns

**10** Cross out the word which does not belong.

1 jam / traffic / lights / ~~person~~

2 car / park / house / rental

3 calling / gift / duty-free / shop

4 industrial / school / housing / estate

5 apartment / primary / language / school

6 one-way / high / news / street

7 shopping / mall / shops / centre

8 semi-detached / flat / terraced / houses

## VOCABULARY the internet

**11 Tick six correct sentences. Correct the wrong sentences.**

1 ~~Blogs~~ *Wikis* are mini-encyclopedias containing useful information.
2 We use search engines to find information quickly.
3 Dating sites contain information about companies and businesses.
4 Wikis tell us which products, films, places, etc. are the best.
5 Photo sharing sites let us upload our pictures so our friends can see them.
6 Ratings sites tell us about individuals – their family, friends and hobbies, etc.
7 News sites tell us what's happening in the world.
8 Social networking sites let us stay in contact with old friends, and make new ones.
9 Travel sites allow us to research places and sometimes book holidays.
10 We use personal homepages to find a partner.
11 Video sharing sites allow people to put film clips on the web.
12 Corporate websites are a type of online journal.

## GRAMMAR relative clauses

**12 Join the sentences using *which, where* or *who*.**

1 I spoke to a doctor. He was very nice.
The doctor _____.
2 We visited a museum. It had a wonderful exhibition.
The museum _____.
3 She was born on an island. It's now under water.
The island _____.
4 My girlfriend is in the fashion industry. She lives in Paris.
My girlfriend, _____.
5 I grew up in a house. It's now a theatre.
The house _____.
6 Tom is my best friend. He works with my father.
Tom, _____.
7 The sale in Macy's lasted for ten days. It's now finished.
The sale in Macy's, _____.
8 They went to a restaurant. It served crocodile.
The restaurant _____.

## VOCABULARY welcoming

**13 Complete the sentences with a suitable verb.**

1 Welcome to the company. Please _____ a seat.
2 You want to use the phone? _____ my guest.
3 Come in. _____ the mess. I've been very busy.
4 Let me take your coat. _____ yourself at home.
5 You look tired. Why don't you _____ your feet up?
6 Hungry? Please _____ yourself.

## FUNCTION being a good guest

**14 Read the conversations. Cross out eleven extra words.**

Conversation 1
Pete: Hi, Don. Is it OK if I ~~to~~ bring a friend to your party?
Don: Yes, of course. No problem.
Pete: Oh, and one other thing. Do I need for to bring anything?
Don: No, it's not the necessary. We have everything we need.

Conversation 2
Joe: I put my feet on the table. Did I do something wrong?
Kat: Oh. It's considered be a bit rude.
Joe: Really? Sorry about that. I didn't know.
Kat: It's OK – we can sort it but out.

Conversation 3
Andre: Is this for a bad time? I can come back later.
Bella: Can you to come back in ten minutes?
Andre: Yes, of course. My apologies. I didn't can realise you were in a meeting.
Bella: It's fine. Don't to worry about it.

Conversation 4
Nick: We caught Roger stealing again. What should we to do?
Tam: If I were you, I'd give him a final warning. You haven't told anyone else?
Nick: No, of course not. OK, I'll do that. Should I tell my boss?
Tam: No, you'd better be not.

## LEARN TO accept apologies

**15 Add the words in the box to the correct place in B's replies in the conversations.**

all right    it's (×2)    no    at    to

1 A: Sorry I didn't bring a dish. I just didn't have time.
B: You really don't have *to* apologise. We weren't expecting anything!
2 A: I'm sorry – I forgot to bring my notes.
B: It's problem. I can photocopy mine.
3 A: Sorry, did I bump you?
B: That's. It didn't hurt.
4 A: Sorry, am I late?
B: Not all. We usually don't start till 3.15.
5 A: Sorry, did I step on your toe?
B: No, nothing. I didn't even feel it.
6 A: I'm so sorry about missing lunch.
B: Honestly, fine. Don't worry about it.

## TEST

**Circle the correct option to complete the sentences.**

1 We're going to focus _____ quality.

  a) to              b) on          c) by

2 For the last two hours _____ in the garden, so I'm tired.

  a) I'm working      b) I work
  c) I've been working

3 Jun and I _____ each other for ten years.

  a) have been knowing   b) have known
  c) are knowing

4 I think I like the new flat, but I _____ there long.

  a) haven't been living   b) am not living
  c) don't live

5 Bad news – his dog _____.

  a) is died        b) has been dying   c) has died

6 We really depend _____ our sponsors.

  a) of             b) to          c) on

7 You have _____ for tennis.

  a) an expert      b) an attitude   c) an aptitude

8 I'm hopeless _____ languages.

  a) in             b) on         c) at

9 Will you _____ finish your work on time?

  a) can           b) be able      c) manage to

10 I'm afraid I _____ to help you.

  a) am unable      b) can't        c) manage

11 When he was three, he _____ already talk.

  a) managed      b) was able     c) could

12 I'm _____ an apprenticeship in an internet company.

  a) doing         b) making      c) working

13 She just got her driving _____.

  a) exam         b) licence      c) certificate

14 In my _____, Tokyo's the world's greatest city.

  a) view         b) opinions     c) thinking

15 Let me _____ you an example of what I mean.

  a) make        b) take        c) give

16 Those people should _____ their own business.

  a) take         b) mind        c) think

17 He's training to become _____.

  a) pilot         b) the pilot     c) a pilot

18 _____ usually start to walk at about twelve months.

  a) Children      b) A child      c) The children

19 There were _____ people at the party.

  a) plenty of      b) a few of     c) lots

20 I ate _____ ice cream, and now I feel sick.

  a) too          b) too much     c) too many

21 We grew up on a _____ estate.

  a) housing       b) house       c) living

22 I often use search _____ to find out information.

  a) machines      b) engines      c) sites

23 I use a video _____ site.

  a) internet       b) loading      c) sharing

24 The road _____ we wanted to take was closed.

  a) that         b) where       c) what

25 Tillie, _____ is already at university.

  a) that's only sixteen,   b) who's only sixteen
  c) who's only sixteen,

26 The town _____ is full of trees.

  a) where I live      b) which I live   c) where, I live

27 Russia, _____ has changed a lot.

  a) which we visited in 1989,
  b) which we visited in 1989
  c) what we visited in 1989,

28 Come in and _____ yourself at home.

  a) be           b) take        c) make

29 My _____. I didn't know you were busy.

  a) disgrace       b) sorry        c) apologies

30 If this is a bad _____, I can come back later.

  a) time         b) hour        c) timing

**TEST RESULT**     **/30**

## VOCABULARY history

**1A Find nouns in the word square that match meanings 1–10.**

1 A complete change either in the way people think, or in a country's political system.

2 The time when an important change begins to happen. (two words)

3 An event that changes a situation, or the process of growing or changing.

4 When something increases and affects more people.

5 Any change, discovery or invention that makes the world better.

6 A group of people that works to achieve an aim.

7 A machine, tool, system, etc., made for the first time.

8 The basic idea or principle behind something.

9 Something that someone learns about when it was not known before.

10 Change that improves something.

| T | U | R | N | I | N | G | P | O | I | N | T |
|---|---|---|---|---|---|---|---|---|---|---|---|
| D | A | E | B | P | R | O | G | R | E | S | S |
| E | C | V | D | E | R | I | O | M | E | I | P |
| V | F | O | U | N | D | A | T | I | O | N | T |
| E | E | L | U | F | C | S | S | G | J | V | E |
| L | S | U | A | V | U | A | P | L | I | E | D |
| O | W | T | V | A | P | D | R | A | G | N | E |
| P | D | I | S | C | O | V | E | R | Y | T | X |
| M | E | O | R | E | K | A | A | E | I | I | H |
| E | D | N | I | U | F | N | D | O | E | O | O |
| N | C | I | N | T | I | C | F | R | S | N | E |
| T | M | O | V | E | M | E | N | T | C | L | F |

**B Underline the correct alternative.**

1 History books say Alexander Fleming was responsible for the *foundation / discovery* of penicillin.

2 The internet has helped the *turning point / spread* of their ideas.

3 After finishing the research, we'll begin work on the *development / advance* of the product.

4 James is making a lot of *progress / discovery* in all his school subjects.

5 There have been amazing *advances / spreads* in technology in the last few years.

6 She was a member of the early feminist *progress / movement*.

7 Only a *foundation / revolution* will destroy this government.

8 I think the wheel is the greatest *invention / movement* in history.

## GRAMMAR third conditional

**2 Circle the correct option to complete the sentences.**

1 They would have said something if we _____ the rules.
   a) were broken   b) would have broken   c) had broken

2 If _____ you, I would have said 'hello'.
   a) I would see   b) I have seen   c) I'd seen

3 He _____ if the ambulance hadn't come.
   a) would died   b) would have died   c) would have been died

4 If I'd known a ticket cost €100, I _____.
   a) wouldn't have come   b) would have came
   c) not would have come

5 She would have arrived at the airport on the wrong day if I _____ her.
   a) haven't phoned   b) hadn't phoned   c) wouldn't phone

6 If the government hadn't lent the company a million pounds, it _____.
   a) had closed   b) would close   c) would have closed

7 They would have had a picnic if it _____.
   a) hadn't rained   b) had rained not   c) had been rained

8 If he hadn't had such a great coach, John wouldn't _____ a great squash player.
   a) have become   b) to become   c) had become

**3 Write a sentence with *if* for situations 1–8.**

1 Early travellers invented boats. Cross-continental travel became possible.

   *If early travellers hadn't invented boats, cross-continental travel wouldn't have become possible.*

2 Archduke Ferdinand was assassinated. World War I started.
   _____

3 People from Sumer needed permanent records. They invented writing. _____

4 World War II happened. The United Nations was formed in 1945.
   _____

5 William the Conqueror invaded England in 1066. The English language changed. _____

6 Charles Darwin travelled to South America. He developed the theory of evolution. _____

7 Sailors on the *Titanic* didn't see the iceberg and 1,595 people died.
   _____

8 Captain James Cook sailed to Australia. It became a British colony.

**4A ▶ 9.1 Listen and add two missing contractions to each sentence.**

1 If I known you were coming, I waited.
   'd           would've

2 If I waited, I been late.

3 If I been late, I missed the show.

4 If I missed the show, I wasted my money.

5 If I wasted my money, I been angry.

**B Listen again and repeat the sentences. Pay attention to the pronunciation of *had* and *would have*.**

## LISTENING

**5A** ▶ 9.2 Look at 1–5 below and think about the question: Where and when were these things first used? Listen and complete the answers.

| Invention | Where? | When? |
|---|---|---|
| 1 toothpaste | _Egypt_ | _1,600_ years ago |
| 2 biological weapons | _____ | _____ years ago |
| 3 football | _____ | _____ years ago |
| 4 central heating | _____ | _____ years ago |
| 5 umbrella | _____ | _____ years ago |

**B** What is the connection between the inventions in Exercise 5A and pictures A–E below? Listen again and check.

**C** Read these extracts from the listening in Exercise 5A and find words to match definitions a)–e) below.

1 Was it the same as modern toothpaste? Definitely not. Ancient Greek toothpaste used ingredients like crushed bones and oyster shells.

2 Some generals would even throw dead bodies at the enemy or into the enemy's river.

3 In the 18th century, one way American Indians were killed was through using infected blankets given to them by the Europeans who were colonising America.

4 A rich banker installed it in his house so that he could grow grapes in England's cold weather!

5 Interestingly, it seems that only kings or very important people had umbrellas in these sculptures. So they were a symbol of high social class.

a) the people that your country is fighting against in a war
_____

b) something that represents a special quality or situation
_____

c) placed somewhere and connected ready to be used
_____

d) containing dangerous bacteria which spread disease
_____

e) pressed very hard so it is broken into extremely small pieces _____

## WRITING a short essay; structuring paragraphs

**6A** Read the introduction to a short essay and choose the best title.

a) Sumerian Culture

b) The History of Writing

c) Business throughout History

In 3200 BC, Sumerians invented writing. For these people, who were located in the area we now call Iraq, there was nothing poetic about it. They didn't write to fire the imagination or to tell beautiful stories. <u>Instead</u>, they wrote because it was a way to keep business records. While previous generations had relied on their memory for the details of deals and the things they owned, the new generation decided to make permanent records. As a result, early 'writing' looks like a very simple type of drawing.

**B** Read the introduction again and:

1 Circle the topic sentence.

2 Underline a linking word (one has already been underlined).

3 Underline one linking expression (three words).

**C** Read the notes and finish the essay (120–150 words).

(Symbols) ------------------------------

At first = pictures of animals, body parts, trees, birds, everyday tools
Then later symbols = for ideas
Then later symbols = for sounds
Could be read left to right or right to left — picture of a head (human or animal) at beginning of line showed readers the direction to read in

(Writing) ------------------------------

On walls of temples and on papyrus (early paper)
99% of people = illiterate — only religious leaders/ scholars read
Start of writing = start of 'history' — ideas and other info passed down through time

## GRAMMAR active versus passive

**1A** Read the text and correct five mistakes with passives.

# WHERE I GREW UP

I grew up in a big old house with a big old family. The house had four floors, one floor for each generation.

The bottom floor was where my maternal grandparents lived. They were give the bottom floor so that they didn't have to climb any steps – that's the story I was told, anyway. But in reality, I think it's because my grandmother escaped the house at 4.00a.m. every morning to go for walks and we didn't want to been woken up.

Mum and Dad's room was on the second floor, and us children were be put on the third floor, out of the way.

At the very top of the steps there was an attic where my great-grandfather was hidden away, out of sight. He was as mad as a box of frogs. He used to play operas on an ancient gramophone and sing Puccini at the top of his voice. When he died, I was given that gramophone and all his records. Amazingly, forty years later, it still works.

The house has be rebuilt many times since those days and the garden, where we used to climb trees and run wild, has been covered with concrete. I read recently that the house will to be sold again. It won't be bought by me, though. My memories are enough.

**B** Read the text again and underline five correct examples of the passive.

**2A** Rewrite sentences 1–8 using passives. Do not say who did the action.

1 People give the Institute almost a million euros a year.
   _The Institute is given almost a million euros a year._

2 One day they will discover a cure for cancer.
   _____

3 Someone stole the files last year.
   _____

4 They took these famous photos at the end of the war.
   _____

5 Nobody has told the President about the plan.
   _____

6 The searchers have found the missing people.
   _____

7 They cancelled all flights going out of Paris.
   _____

8 Someone cleans the paintings once a year.
   _____

**B** ▶ 9.3 Listen and check. What happens to the pronunciation of the auxiliary verbs *are*, *were*, *has(n't) been* and *have been*? Listen again and repeat.

## VOCABULARY periods of time

**3** Replace the underlined phrases with the phrases in the box.

> the generation    over a quarter-century    millennium
> just over a century ago    era    half a century
> over seven decades    just over a fortnight

1 The 18<sup>th</sup> century was a great *era* period of time for music.

2 Nelson Mandela spent twenty-seven years in prison.

3 In 1909, Geronimo, the Native American leader, died.

4 We are in the first stage of a new thousand-year cycle.

5 Louis XIV ruled France for seventy-two years.

6 A world full of technology is normal for those people born in the 1990s.

7 Jack Kerouac wrote *On the Road*, a classic novel about 1960s freedom, in about eighteen days.

8 Fidel Castro led Cuba for nearly fifty years.

## VOCABULARY PLUS collocations with
*come, give, have* and *make*

**4A** Complete phrases 1–16 with *come, give, have* or *make*. Use each verb four times.

| | | | |
|---|---|---|---|
| 1 | _____ a good time | 9 | _____ directions |
| 2 | _____ progress | 10 | _____ trouble |
| 3 | _____ a talk | 11 | _____ back |
| 4 | _____ naturally | 12 | _____ a mess |
| 5 | _____ a break | 13 | _____ me a call |
| 6 | _____ a dream | 14 | _____ a profit |
| 7 | _____ first | 15 | _____ by car |
| 8 | _____ instructions | 16 | _____ a decision |

**B** Complete 1–5 using two collocations with the same verb. Make sure you use the correct tense.

1 I'm _____ _____ with this report. It's really difficult to write. I think I'll _____ a _____ and finish it later.

2 In 1998, the company _____ a _____ to close its European offices. After two years, it _____ a _____ of over $1,000,000.

3 Can you _____ me a _____ when you get this message? I need you to _____ me _____ to your house. I'm completely lost!

4 Drawing didn't _____ _____ to me. It took me years to become good at it, but last year I _____ _____ in an art competition.

5 The boss is going to _____ a _____ to the employees next week. He wants to _____ _____ on how to use the new software.

## READING

**5A** Look at the table. What information do you think goes in gaps 1–6? Read the text below and check your ideas.

| Four Generations | | | |
| --- | --- | --- | --- |
| **Name:** | **Born:** | **Origin of name:** | **Known for:** |
| The Lost Generation | 1_____ | Gertrude Stein, a writer, named them. | Millions died in World War I (1914–1918) |
| Baby Boomers | 2_____ | The 'baby boom' (high birth rates) after World War II | Being successful (in USA) |
| Generation X | 1960s and 1970s | 3_____ | 4_____ |
| Millennials (Generation Y) | 5_____ | A book: *Millennials Rising: The Next Great Generation* | 6_____ |

# Generations and Generalisations

'Young people these days! They contradict their parents, chatter in the company of guests, eat their food too quickly, and are rude to their teachers!' Who said this? Was it a tired, stressed twenty-first century parent? No. These words were said by Socrates in Athens two and a half thousand years ago. It seems that every generation complains about the next generation. But now there's another element: in the twentieth century we began naming each generation.

First came The Lost Generation (born around 1880–1895). This was the generation which fought in World War I (1914–1918), in which over fifteen million people were killed. American writer Gertrude Stein is famous for naming it The Lost Generation, but actually it was her French car mechanic (she lived in Paris) who first used the expression. He complained that the young mechanics who worked for him were useless at their jobs, and he described them as *une génération perdue* – a lost generation! Stein borrowed the expression.

After the Second World War, there was the Boomer Generation, or the Baby Boomers. This was the generation born between 1945 and about 1960, a period when birth rates increased throughout the world. In the USA, the Baby Boomers are seen as the great, successful generation which made their country rich.

The next generation was called Generation X. The name was popularised by Canadian writer Douglas Coupland in his 1991 novel, *Generation X: Tales for an Accelerated Culture*. People from Generation X – born in the 1960s and 1970s – rebelled against their parents' values. They didn't want to work for the same company their whole life, and they spent their time listening to 'grunge' music or playing video games.

The next generation has two names: Generation Y and the Millennials. Generation Y was first described in detail in 2000, when Neil Howe and William Strauss wrote *Millennials Rising: The Next Great Generation*. Generation Y – people who were born in the 1980s and 1990s – is known for its love of technology: iPods, mobile phones, digital cameras, digital everything. They are amazing networkers, constantly online, and great multi-taskers. They can read (web pages), listen (to music on their iPods) and write (Instant Messages) all at the same time.

But are these generational names correct? Can we really describe a whole generation as having similar habits and qualities? How similar are the lives of teenagers in New York to the lives of teenagers in rural China or Peru? In 2010, only a quarter of the world's population used the internet. Only a small percentage of those had iPods. So can we say this generation loves technology?

Are we really talking about generations or generalisations?

**B** Complete the questions.

1 Q: What did _____?
   A: 'Young people these days! They contradict their parents, chatter in the company of guests, eat their food too quickly, and are rude to their teachers!'

2 Q: When did we _____?
   A: In the twentieth century.

3 Q: How many _____?
   A: Over fifteen million.

4 Q: What happened _____?
   A: Birth rates increased throughout the world.

5 Q: Who _____?
   A: Neil Howe and William Strauss.

6 Q: How many _____?
   A: Twenty-five percent of the world's population.

**C** Match words 1–6 with definitions a)–f).

1 contradict (line 1)
2 chatter (line 1)
3 birth rate (line 20)
4 popularise (line 25)
5 networkers (line 37)
6 multi-taskers (line 38)

a) make something known and liked by many people
b) people who spend a lot of time communicating and sharing information with others
c) the number of children born in a particular year/place
d) talk quickly in a friendly way about unimportant things
e) disagree, saying that the opposite is true
f) people who can do lots of things at the same time

# HISTORY NOW MAGAZINE ASKS 'WHO DO YOU ADMIRE?'

'I admire the explorer Ranulph Fiennes. He walked to both the South and North Poles, crossed Antarctica on foot, and climbed Mount Everest when he was sixty-five. He lost fingers and toes and still kept exploring. You have to be [1]b__ _v__ to do that. He's very [2]ch__ _ _ _m_ _ _ _ too: he was on a shortlist to play James Bond, but Roger Moore got the part instead! Fiennes's life has been [3]ex_ _ _ _ _ _y; one of his greatest achievements is that he has raised over 5 million pounds for charity.'

(Mark, climber)

'I admire Wangari Maathai. She's a Kenyan activist who founded The Green Belt Movement, an organisation that protects the environment. She has also been very [4]i_f_ _ _ _ _ _ _l in the women's rights movement. She was the first African woman to win the Nobel Peace Prize, which, for women all over the world, is absolutely [5]i_ _p_ _ _ _ _ _n_ _. It shows that women in poor countries can make a difference.'

(Umunyana, teacher)

'I love Ang Lee's films. I think he's the most [6]cr_ _ _ _ _ _ director working today. I've watched *Crouching Tiger, Hidden Dragon* seven times. I love the shots of landscapes and people flying through the air. It just seems so [7]o_ _ _ _ _ _l compared to most Hollywood films. His films are always really [8]i_ _ _ _ _ _ _v_ too – like *Brokeback Mountain*. Who could imagine a story about gay cowboys becoming a classic?'

(Hae Jin, film student)

## VOCABULARY describing people

**1** Read the text and complete words 1–8.

## FUNCTION expressing uncertainty

**2** Circle the correct option to complete the conversations.

1  A: When were the first Olympic Games?
   B: a) I have no idea.
      b) I haven't got an idea.

2  A: Do you know who invented the machine gun?
   B: a) I haven't the clue.
      b) I haven't a clue.

3  A: What's the world's biggest country?
   B: a) I'm not a hundred percent certain, and it might be Russia.
      b) I'm not a hundred percent certain, but it might be Russia.

4  A: Do you know when the first emails were sent?
   B: a) I'm fairly sure it was in the 1970s.
      b) I'm fair sure it was in the 1970s.

5  A: Who's the current President of South Africa?
   B: a) It's definitely but not Thabo Mbeki.
      b) It's definitely not Thabo Mbeki.

6  A: Which country has reached the World Cup final the most times?
   B: a) I don't know, but I'm sure it isn't England.
      b) I don't know, but I've sure it isn't England.

7  A: What year did Yuri Gagarin fly into space?
   B: a) I don't can remember.
      b) I can't remember.

8  A: What's the name of that French woman who lived to 122?
   B: a) I've forgotten.
      b) I'm forgotten.

## LEARN TO react to information

**3A** Complete the conversations.

1  A: Marisa had her baby yesterday.
   B: _____ she? What wonderful news!

2  A: I'm doing an online project about Second Life.
   B: Oh really? _____'s interesting.

3  A: His cousin was an Olympic boxer.
   B: _____ he? Wow!

4  A: My sister doesn't eat meat.
   B: _____ she? OK, I'll cook fish.

5  A: The King of Italy? There isn't one! Italy is a republic.
   B: I was just about to _____ that.

6  A: I love Lady Gaga!
   B: _____ you? I think she's crazy.

7  A: The inventor of the internet? It was Tim Berners-Lee.
   B: Oh yes, I knew that. I just couldn't _____.

8  A: My parents have never been here.
   B: _____ they? When are they going to visit?

9  A: Jake was the number one student in the country.
   B: Really? I _____ know that.

10 A: John's got the car. We'll have to travel by bus.
   B: _____ we? Oh, that's annoying.

**B** ▶ 9.4 Listen and check. Then listen again and shadow B's part. Try to copy the intonation.

## VOCABULARY the environment

**1A** Put the letters in the box in the correct order to make words and phrases. Then match them with definitions 1–10.

> scoredspe   no tabysdn   gicanpagk
> negery-vangis   naricog   ecdosn-danh
> lebodu gezald   celedrcy   rep-peerdarp
> dnsuiltea

1 not switched off, but ready to be used when needed _____

2 windows or doors with two layers of glass _____

3 food with substances added to it in order to preserve it, improve its colour, etc. _____

4 covered with a material that stops electricity, sound, heat, etc. from getting out _____

5 grown without chemicals _____

6 food which has already been washed, prepared, cooked, etc. so that it is ready to eat _____

7 the bags, boxes, etc. that a product is sold in _____

8 using less electricity than normal _____

9 glass or paper, etc. which has been processed so that it can be used again _____

10 not new; has been owned by someone else _____

**B** Complete the sentences with words from Exercise 1A.

1 We don't use chemicals. All our fruit and vegetables are _____.

2 I don't buy new clothes – I buy everything from _____ shops.

3 All the windows are _____ so we can't hear the noise outside.

4 If we changed to _____ light bulbs, our electricity bills would be cheaper.

5 I don't have time to cook in the evenings, so I buy a _____ meal on the way home.

6 Everything in the café is fresh and natural. We don't use any _____ food.

7 All the paper and plastic from the office is _____ in these bins.

8 Don't leave the TV on _____. Turn it off when you go to bed.

9 I don't buy fruit in the supermarket because they use too much _____ which can't be recycled.

10 The house is much warmer now that we have _____ the roof.

## LISTENING

**2A** Read the text about Earth Hour. Can you complete it?

> ### EARTH HOUR: HOW SMALL ACTIONS CAN HAVE A BIG IMPACT
>
> Earth Hour is a global event where people around the world switch off the $^1$_____ in their houses, offices, and at other important landmarks, like the $^2$_____ in Paris, and the $^3$_____ in Egypt. It started in 2007 in $^4$_____, Australia, as a protest against climate $^5$_____, and has grown into a world-wide event. But not everyone thinks it is a good idea – people have $^6$_____ opinions about what an event like Earth Hour can achieve.

**B** ▶10.1 Listen to a radio phone-in programme about Earth Hour and see if you were right.

**3A** Are the statements true (T) or false (F)? Correct the false statements.

1 In 2007, twenty-two million people across Sydney switched off their lights for Earth Hour.

2 In 2010, thousands of cities in 128 countries took part in the event.

3 Organisers say that they want to show what people can do to save energy.

4 Everybody agrees that the event is a good way to help people understand the problem.

5 Amy and her children had dinner by candlelight.

6 Jay-Jay thinks that the event helps people to change their everyday behaviour.

**B** Complete the phrases in bold so that they mean the same as the phrase in brackets.

1 One city decided to **take a _____ against** climate change. (protest against)

2 Earth Hour quickly **went _____.** (spread across the world)

3 In 2010, thousands of cities in 128 countries **took _____.** (participated)

4 The Eiffel Tower in Paris, the Egyptian Pyramids, New York's Empire State Building and Sydney Harbour Bridge were all _____ **into darkness.** (made to go dark quickly)

5 Organisers want to **draw _____ to** the problem of climate change. (make people notice)

6 Is it a good way to **_____ awareness** about the problems the world is facing? (increase the number of people who know about something)

7 I think it's a **complete _____ of time.** (not a good way to use time)

## GRAMMAR reported speech

**4 Complete the reported sentences.**

1 'I don't understand why you're always late.'

She said that she _____ understand why I was always late.

2 'We're meeting outside the gym at 6.15,' Bill told the others.

Bill said that they _____ meeting outside the gym at 6.15.

3 'I've eaten plenty already, thank you.'

He said that he _____ eaten plenty already.

4 'My job finished last week,' she told Jim.

She told Jim that _____ job had finished the week before.

5 'I'll see you tomorrow,' said Adam.

Adam said that he would see us the _____ day.

6 'It's my favourite programme.'

Luis told his mother that it was _____ favourite programme.

7 'We'll meet you at the airport.'

They told her that they _____ meet her at the airport.

8 'Are you enjoying the trip?' the tour leader asked.

The tour leader asked them if _____ were enjoying the trip.

**5A** Ali (A) is talking to a travel agent (T) about booking a holiday. Put their conversation in the correct order.

A: ___ No, I haven't, but it's a good idea.

A: _1_ I want to go to Spain, because I've never been there before.

A: ___ OK.

A: ___ I'm thinking of going by plane.

A: ___ That sounds great!

A: ___ No, I haven't. Could you show me what accommodation is available?

T: ___ Have you thought about taking the train instead?

T: ___ How are you planning to travel?

T: ___ There's an eco-farm near Valencia where you can stay for free, if you help the farmer pick his olives.

T: ___ It's cheaper than flying. I'll show you some of the train routes.

T: ___ Have you decided where you want to stay?

**B Complete the sentences reporting the conversation in Exercise 5A. Write one word in each gap. Contractions are one word.**

1 Ali said that _she_ _wanted_ to go to Spain because _she'd_ _never_ _been_ _there_ before.

2 The travel agent _____ _____ how she _____ _____ to travel.

3 She said that _____ _____ _____ of going by plane.

4 He asked her if _____ _____ about taking the train instead.

5 Ali said that _____ _____, but that _____ _____ a good idea.

6 The travel agent said that it was cheaper than flying, and that he _____ _____ _____ some of the train routes.

7 He asked her if she _____ _____ where _____ _____ to stay.

8 She said that _____ _____. She asked him to show her what accommodation was available.

9 He said that there was an eco-farm near Valencia where she _____ _____ for free, if she _____ the farmer pick his olives.

10 Ali said that _____ _____.

## VOCABULARY PLUS word-building (prefixes)

**6 Add prefixes un-, dis-, over-, under-, mis- or re- to the words in bold to complete the sentences.**

1 I _____**understood** his directions and got completely lost.

2 Discipline is very important to us. We don't like the children to _____**obey** the teacher.

3 Shall I throw these boxes away, or can we _____**use** them for something else?

4 It's a very _____**usual** situation. Nothing like this has happened before.

5 I _____**estimated** how long the journey would take. It took an hour longer than I expected.

6 The old man walked around the corner, and _____**appeared**. We never saw him again.

7 I don't know how you find anything in this office. It's so _____**tidy**!

8 I have to _____**new** my driving licence because it has expired.

9 They use children in their factories, which I find completely _____**ethical**.

10 I'm afraid I have to _____**agree**. I don't think that's right at all.

## VOCABULARY reporting verbs

**1** Circle the correct option to complete the reported statements.

1 'Can I give you a hand?'

He _____ to help.

a) invited   b) refused   c) offered

2 'I'm afraid the first train leaves at 6.30a.m.'

She _____ that the first train leaves at 6.30a.m.

a) offered   b) explained   c) suggested

3 'I don't believe you!'

He _____ to believe me.

a) refused   b) promised   c) offered

4 'Come in and have something to eat.'

She _____ us in for something to eat.

a) offered   b) warned   c) invited

5 'Don't go there. It's dangerous.'

He _____ us not to go there.

a) warned   b) suggested   c) invited

6 'I'll buy you a diamond ring.'

He _____ to buy me a diamond ring.

a) explained   b) promised   c) suggested

7 'Why don't we go for a walk?'

He _____ going for a walk.

a) warned   b) offered   c) suggested

## READING

**2** Read the article and match pictures A–E with paragraphs 1–5.

## A TASTE OF YOUR LIFE

**1** In the BBC chat show series *A Taste of My Life*, TV chef Nigel Slater talks to celebrities about their strongest food memories, and particular dishes which have shaped their lives. Comic actor Sanjeev Bhaskar **reminisces** about the contrast between bland 'meat and two veg' school dinners and the Indian food he was served at home. Fellow chef Nigella Lawson tells her life story through food. Do you have a memory of a favourite dish, associated with a special event? Can you remember who cooked it? We asked for your best food memories.

**2** It has to be **boiled** eggs with 'soldiers'. My mum used to give this to us as kids. The egg should be soft-boiled so the **yolk** is still **runny**, and the toast is spread with melted butter, and cut into thin strips (tall and straight, like soldiers), which you can hold and dip into the top of the egg. Now I give it to my kids and they love it. It's healthy, and I hope it will give them the same happy memories. *Claire, UK*

**3** My grandmother's homemade pasta. She used to make pasta on the kitchen table every day. I can remember her laying out the pasta in the morning when I got up for breakfast. Nowadays, people have pasta machines, but she would roll out the pasta by hand, and when we came home from school, there was always a plate of fresh **tagliatelle** waiting for us. The dry pasta you buy in the shops just doesn't taste the same. *Mariella, Italy*

**4** Tortilla. Whenever I feel like I'm missing my home country, I cook a tortilla. It's a kind of omelette made with potato and onion, and you can find it in all the tapas bars in Spain. But, of course, the one I make at home is the best. I have so many happy memories of eating tortilla. They go all through my life, from when I was a child, a student at university, eating with friends. Tortilla is everywhere. I couldn't live without it. *Jorge, Spain*

**5** When I go back to Penang (Malaysia), I go straight to a hawker (street/café seller) and order a bowl of Penang Hokkien Mee (Prawn Noodle Soup). It's one dish I always **miss**. There is something about the combination of the prawns and the chilli in the soup, with the noodles. I just love it. You can make it at home too, but it tastes better when you eat it out on the street. There's an atmosphere, with the heat, and the noise of the traffic and people shouting. It's more than just a dish – it's an experience. And I always look forward to it. Penang's food is part of my life. In fact, I don't think you can find the same taste anywhere else. *Irene, US*

**3** Read the article again and answer the questions.

1 Who has happy memories of the dish from different stages of their life?

_____

2 Who likes to eat this dish when they return to a special place?

_____

3 Who wants to feed her children a dish which her mother fed her as a child? _____

4 Who describes how the dish should be prepared? _____

5 Who remembers eating this dish when they came home from school as a child? _____

6 Who thinks the dish tastes better when you eat in on the street?

_____

**4** Underline the correct alternative for these words and phrases from the article.

1 reminisces: talk or think about *pleasant / terrible* events in your past

2 boiled: cooked in *oil / water*

3 yolk: the *yellow middle / shell* of an egg

4 runny: *hard / soft; liquid*

5 tagliatelle: a type of *pasta / soup*

6 miss: feel *sad because you haven't got / happy because you have got* something you like

## GRAMMAR verb patterns

**5** Complete the email with verb patterns which include the verbs in brackets. You may need to add personal pronouns (e.g. *us, me*).

Hi Francesca,

How are things? We've just had a great weekend. Ali and Greg are over from New Zealand, so we ¹*decided to meet* (decide/meet) up. They wanted to see London, so I ²_____ (suggest/spend) a couple of days there. Louise ³_____ (invite/stay) at her place, which made things easier. She also ⁴_____ (offer/take) some time off work, so she could show us around the sights. She ⁵_____ (explain/be) easier to travel around with someone who knows where everything is. We were planning to get an organised bus tour, but Louise ⁶_____ (recommend/travel) by ourselves on the buses and Underground. It was a great way to see the city. There were so many things we all wanted to see, but we ⁷_____ (agree/choose) one or two things each. I was really keen to go on the London Eye, but Louise ⁸_____ (warn/not go) up because the weather was bad. We saw lots of other things though, like Big Ben and the Tate Modern. I ⁹_____ (promise/write) and tell you all about it. Next time, you must come, too!

Hope you're well. Take care.

Matt

**6A** Complete the second sentence so that it has the same meaning as the first. Use the words in capitals. Use between two and five words.

1 'I'm not coming with you,' said Gina. REFUSE
  Gina _____ with us.

2 'I'll definitely call you later,' he said. PROMISE
  He _____ me later.

3 'Let's go out for a meal,' they said. DECIDE
  They _____ out for a meal.

4 'OK. We won't go on holiday this year,' they said. AGREE
  They _____ on holiday this year.

5 'It's a very expensive restaurant,' she told us. WARN
  She _____ the restaurant was very expensive.

6 'James, why don't you come to the theatre with us on Friday?' they asked. INVITE
  They _____ to the theatre with them on Friday.

7 'The children grow vegetables in the garden.' EXPLAIN
  The teacher _____ grow vegetables in the garden.

8 'You should buy your fruit at the market.' RECOMMEND
  He _____ our fruit at the market.

**B** ▶ 10.2 Listen and check. Then listen and repeat. What happens to the words *to, for, at* and *that* in the sentences? Are they stressed or unstressed?

## WRITING a review; linking ideas

**7A** Read the review. Does the writer recommend the restaurant? Why/Why not?

**TIFFANY'S** | PINE WOODS, 0465 244 963

A colleague of mine recommended Tiffany's. Perhaps I should just say that I won't be following his recommendations any more. As I walked in, the first things I noticed were the large flat-screen TVs all over the restaurant, each one showing a different football game. ¹_____. My first reaction was to walk straight out, but there were quite a lot of people there, and we were hungry, so we decided to stay and see what the food was like.

First of all, we ordered drinks. When they arrived, the waitress had forgotten the water, none of the drinks had ice, and ²_____. We didn't see the waitress again for about another twenty minutes. When she finally reappeared, we tried to order some food. I was amazed when she didn't even write down our order. ³_____. I'm sorry, but a good waiter/waitress will always write down what you want.

The starters arrived, but they were very small. ⁴_____. I ate it, but it was nothing special. If you're looking for somewhere nice to eat, then I wouldn't choose Tiffany's, ⁵_____.

**B** Complete phrases a)–e) with the words in the box. Then match them with gaps 1–5 in the review.

unless    such    so    while    although    that

a) ... one of the glasses was _____ dirty that we sent it back.

b) _____ the main courses were a little better, my fish was fried, and not grilled as I had asked for.

c) ... _____ you just want to enjoy the football.

d) She thought she had _____ a good memory _____ she would remember everything.

e) _____ the décor was bright and fun-looking, the atmosphere was uninviting, and the chairs weren't comfortable at all.

**8A** Read the review again and tick the information it gives. Which information is <u>not</u> given?

1 information about the price
2 information about the menu and type of food served
3 details of the restaurant (name, location, phone number, etc.)
4 information about the service
5 information about the atmosphere

**B** Write a review of a restaurant that someone has recommended to you (180–220 words). Try to include all the information in Exercise 8A.

## VOCABULARY airports

**1** Add vowels to complete the words in the texts.

'I was travelling from Italy to Stockholm for work. In a hurry, I picked up my ¹p__ssp__rt and ticket, and left for the airport without checking them. When I went to ²ch__ck __n my bags, instead of asking me if I wanted an ³__ __sl__ or a window seat, and giving me my ⁴b__ __rd__ng c__rd, the lady behind the desk told me I was at the wrong airport! How was I to know that there were two airports in Milan? I was in the wrong one.'

'I couldn't believe what was happening, when I tried to fly to Houston with my son last month. We had just been through the ⁵X-r__y m__ch__n__ when we were stopped by security guards and told we were not allowed to ⁶b__ __rd the plane. The reason? My son's name, Matthew Gardner, was on a list of wanted criminals. The unbelievable thing is that my son is two years old. Apparently he was 'wanted' in connection with a shooting!'

'While waiting for a connecting flight at Hong Kong airport, I decided to do some shopping. I had a ⁷pr__ __ r__ty b__ __rd__ng card, but I forgot to keep my eye on the departure boards. One minute before my flight was due to leave, I realised to my horror that the message on the departure board read 'Flight XYZ to London – Please ⁸pr__c__ __d t__ g__t__ n__mb__r 143. Final call.' I grabbed my ⁹h__nd l__gg__g__ and ran to the gate like a marathon runner. When I boarded the plane, everyone was staring at me. As if that wasn't bad enough, when I finally found my seat, I realised I'd left my shopping bags, with my new $250 camera in it, in the duty-free shop!'

## FUNCTION giving advice/warnings

**2** Circle the correct option to complete the warnings/advice.

1 Watch _____ for crocodiles. The river is full of them.
   a) up                  b) out
   c) at

2 Don't walk around outside without a sunhat, _____ sunstroke.
   a) or to get           b) or you will getting
   c) or else you'll get

3 Make _____ plenty of water with you. You'll be thirsty by the time you get to the top.
   a) sure you take       b) sure of taking
   c) be sure to

4 _____ leave your bags here, and we'll bring them up for you.
   a) You will better     b) You'd better
   c) You're better

5 If I were you, _____ the airport to see if the flight has been delayed.
   a) I'm calling         b) I'll call
   c) I'd call

6 Be _____ your hand luggage and make sure there are no sharp objects.
   a) careful to check    b) careful and checking
   c) careless and check

7 _____ book a taxi to pick you up from the airport.
   a) Don't forget        b) Don't forget to
   c) Do you forget

8 _____, don't forget your phrasebook. You'll need it if you can't speak the language.
   a) Whatever you do     b) What you do
   c) Ever what you do

## LEARN TO make generalisations

**3** Match 1–6 with a)–f) to make generalisations.

1 Italians have a tendency
2 Generally, people eat
3 English people often
4 In Turkey, it's common to find
5 On the whole, grandparents in China
6 In Latin cultures, the family tends to

a) later in Spain.
b) be very important.
c) to drink coffee, not tea.
d) different styles of cooking in different parts of the country.
e) are very involved in bringing up their grandchildren.
f) complain about the weather.

## VOCABULARY history

**1  Complete the words in these sentences.**

1  The government was removed during the rev_____.

2  The change to farming communities was history's greatest tur_____ p_____.

3  Rich countries should help poor countries in their economic dev_____.

4  Because people lived close together, the disease quickly spr_____.

5  In the fight to cure cancer, the result of this research is a great adv_____.

6  She was one of the most important people in the women's mov_____.

7  The personal computer was the twentieth century's best inv_____.

8  The invention of the wheel provided the fou_____ for most machines.

9  The 3,000-year-old body found in the mountains was a great dis_____.

10  In the debate about climate change, we haven't made much pro_____.

## GRAMMAR third conditional

**2  Complete the sentences with the third conditional form of the verbs in brackets.**

1  If Xiulin _____ (not help) us, we _____ (finish) the project on time.

2  They _____ (go) for a picnic if it _____ (not rain).

3  If I _____ (study), I _____ (not fail) the test.

4  My wife _____ (tell) me if she _____ (have) a problem.

5  If Thierry _____ (not score) that goal, we _____ (not won).

6  What _____ (you/do) if you _____ (miss) the plane?

## GRAMMAR active versus passive

**3  Rewrite the sentences using the passive.**

1  We sell chairs and tables here.
Chairs and tables _____.

2  They don't produce coffee in England.
Coffee _____.

3  They are building a new school.
A new school _____.

4  Someone assassinated the President.
The President _____.

5  Samuel Beckett didn't write *Ulysses*.
*Ulysses* _____.

6  No one has told us anything about the exam.
We _____.

## VOCABULARY periods of time

**4  Underline the correct alternative.**

1  There was a big party to celebrate the new *millennium / fortnight / seventies*.

2  I stayed for *the eighties / a generation / a decade*, arriving in 1989 and leaving in 1999.

3  In the first part of July, we spent *an era / a fortnight / the century* in Greece, on holiday.

4  She worked in the same school for nearly *an age / the nineties / a quarter-century*.

5  War was a way of life for my grandfather's *generation / decade / age*.

6  I grew up in *a century / an era / the nineties*.

## VOCABULARY PLUS collocations with come, give, have and make

**5  Cross out the word which is <u>not</u> possible.**

1  The team came *first / by car / well*.

2  I listened while Sam gave *directions / a discussion / instructions*.

3  William made *project / progress / a mess* in his art class.

4  I had a *dream / homework / good time* last night.

5  My ability to speak French came *naturally / forward / back* to me.

6  She's going to give *a talk / me a call / problem* today.

7  The company has to make a *profit / money / decision*.

8  She sometimes has *progress / trouble / a break* while doing her homework.

## VOCABULARY describing people

**6  Put the letters in bold in the correct order to complete the sentences.**

1  I like **tearceiv** _____ people who have their own ideas.

2  She wasn't very **igolirna** _____; her ideas were nothing new.

3  Like most great leaders, he's very **arccisahtmi** _____.

4  Her life, spent helping others, was **xaeeyplrm** _____.

5  She had some **nnvvatiioe** _____ ideas about design.

6  Like many soldiers, he was extremely **reabv** _____.

7  My boss is **spiirotilnnaa** _____ – everyone follows him.

8  Jackson is the most **neflliunati** _____ player in the team.

## FUNCTION expressing uncertainty

**7** Make sentences with a word or phrase from each section.

| | | |
|---|---|---|
| 1 I've | a) sure | i) clue. |
| 2 I haven't | b) forgotten | ii) isn't Elizabeth. |
| 3 I'm fairly | c) a | iii) it's Jane. |
| 4 It's | d) it | iv) not Sarah. |
| 5 I'm sure | e) no | v) her name. |
| 6 I have | f) definitely | vi) idea. |

1 _I've forgotten her name._

2 _____

3 _____

4 _____

5 _____

6 _____

## LEARN TO react to information

**8** Underline the correct alternative.

1 A: This film is very similar to his last one.
   B: I was *about just / just about* to say that.

2 A: Jeanette Winterson is the one who wrote *The Passion*.
   B: *Does / Is* she? I didn't know that.

3 A: It took over a hundred years to complete the building.
   B: Did it? That's *interesting / too interesting*.

4 A: *Whole Lotta Love* was written by Led Zeppelin.
   B: I knew that. I just *don't / couldn't* remember.

## VOCABULARY the environment

**9** Complete the sentences with the words in the box.

packaging   double glazed   recycled   energy-saving
pre-prepared   on standby   ~~processed~~   insulated
organic   second-hand

1 We try not to eat too much *processed* food, and we grow our own _____ food.

2 We are very conscious of the environment: we use _____ light bulbs and the house is _____.

3 We don't waste energy. Our windows are _____ and we make sure our computers are _____ or switched off.

4 We rarely buy _____ food. The _____ is such a waste of plastic.

5 All of our clothes are _____, and most of our furniture is _____.

## GRAMMAR reported speech

**10** Complete the conversations. B always remembers that A said the opposite earlier.

1 A: That book is very good.
   B: Oh? I thought you said *that book wasn't very good.*

2 A: I know the answer.
   B: Oh? I thought you said _____.

3 A: I haven't been to Germany.
   B: Oh? I thought you said _____.

4 A: I can't swim.
   B: Oh? I thought you said _____.

5 A: I'm going to university.
   B: Oh? I thought you said _____.

6 A: I won't be there on Monday.
   B: Oh? I thought you said _____.

7 A: I'll be able to help.
   B: Oh? I thought you said _____.

8 A: I spoke to Kevin.
   B: Oh? I thought you said _____.

**11** Find and correct five mistakes in the reported questions below.

1 He asked me when started the game.

2 He asked me if I do play any instruments.

3 She asked me where my husband was.

4 She asked me if I worked at home.

5 He asked me why was I crying.

6 She asked me if slept my baby all night.

7 She asked me if they did speak English.

## VOCABULARY PLUS prefixes

**12** Add prefixes to two words in each sentence.

1 Ah, I~~/~~understood the instructions; I thought it was~~/~~usual to cook pasta for forty minutes! *(mis) (un)*

2 He judged the cooking time and left the food in the oven too long; now it's cooked.

3 The results of his diet are believable; he used to be weight, but now he looks fit.

4 The kitchen was tidy so I told her to put things in order, but she obeyed me and went out.

5 We use plastic plates instead of throwing them away, and we cycle food packaging.

6 I approved of Dr Kim's behaviour because it's ethical to give bad advice to patients.

7 Don't estimate the time it takes to new a passport; mine took over two months.

8 He was living here, then he suddenly appeared; at the moment his location is known.

## VOCABULARY reporting verbs

**13** Underline one incorrect verb in each sentence. Which sentence does it belong to?

1 David <u>promised</u> us to his birthday party. *Sentence 6*
2 The tour guide refused us about poisonous spiders.
3 The doorman suggested to let me into the club because I was wearing jeans.
4 I explained to take her for dinner, to say 'thank you'.
5 The teacher invited the grammar clearly so everyone understood.
6 My dad warned to buy me an ice cream if I behaved well.
7 Minty offered going to Greece for our holiday.

## GRAMMAR verb patterns

**14** Underline the correct alternatives.

### World Food restaurant (15 DELANEY ST, SANTA CLARA, 22187)

A friend suggested ¹*for me / that I / me to* go to World Food, and explained ²*me / that / if* I would love the cool, relaxed atmosphere and the outstanding menu. He warned ³*me to / that I / me* expect a big bill at the end, but promised ⁴*me / to / which* that it was worth it.

I arrived at 7.25 for a 7.30 reservation and the receptionist told me ⁵*waiting / wait / to wait* in the bar. I waited for thirty-five minutes before a waiter, with no apology, offered ⁶*for take / taking / to take* me to my table.

The decor was horrible – grey paintings that looked like something your dog might bring home – and I was seated under a speaker playing loud music. I asked the waiter ⁷*give / for give / to give* me a better seat. At first he refused ⁸*to move / moving / move* me, saying the restaurant was full, but finally he agreed ⁹*for / that he / to* give me a window seat.

After the terrible service, I feared the worst, but the food was excellent. My friend had recommended ¹⁰*to try / by trying / trying* the salmon in teriyaki sauce. It was a great choice, as was the apple pie I had for dessert. All World Food needs is a new attitude; the cooking is outstanding.

## VOCABULARY airports

**15** Match 1–8 with a)–h) to make sentences you hear at an airport.

1 May I see
2 Please proceed
3 Is this hand
4 Would you like to check
5 15D is an aisle
6 Your flight will
7 Can I see your boarding
8 We don't have a gate

a) to gate number 62.
b) seat, sir.
c) card, please?
d) your passport, please?
e) luggage, madam?
f) number yet.
g) in this bag?
h) board at 2.45.

## FUNCTION giving advice/warnings

**16** Put the words in italics in the correct order to complete the sentences.

**Q** I'm exploring the Amazon for a few weeks. Can you give me some advice?

**A** OK, ¹*thing is the important to most* _____ be prepared. Read about the Amazon first. Regarding clothes, ²*sure bring you make* _____ a raincoat as it's very wet. Obviously, it's really wild so ³*snakes watch for out* _____. The truth is ⁴*common not very it's* _____ for people to die from snakebites in the Amazon, but it does happen.

**Q** I'm climbing Mount Kilimanjaro. Any tips?

**A** Kilimanjaro is a tough climb, so ⁵*I you, if start I'd were* _____ preparing physically four months before the trip. Also, ⁶*bring to need you* _____ a really good pair of hiking boots. Finally, climbers ⁷*bring tendency a to have* _____ too much stuff. ⁸*you pack don't do, Whatever* _____ too much. You'll have to carry it all up the mountain.

**Q** I'm travelling around India. Can you give me some advice?

**A** Firstly, you'll see some amazing sights, so ⁹*bring forget don't to* _____ a camera. Secondly, ¹⁰*whole the on* _____ Indian food is wonderful, but ¹¹*eat careful be to* _____ only food that has been prepared properly in a kitchen. Also, ¹²*some take better you'd* _____ water-purifying pills because the water can be contaminated.

## TEST

**Circle the correct option to complete the sentences.**

1 The _____ of penicillin was an accident.

   a) discovery       b) discoverer     c) discover

2 Because of the internet, ideas _____ quickly.

   a) revolution      b) invent         c) spread

3 He wouldn't have survived if he _____ his medicine.

   a) took            b) hadn't taken   c) hasn't taken

4 If you had seen her, what _____?

   a) did you say     b) would you said
   c) would you have said

5 If I _____ that it was so hard, I would have asked for help.

   a) would have known  b) knew         c) had known

6 She would _____ famous if she'd been born in another generation.

   a) have be         b) have been      c) had been

7 All articles _____ by our board of editors.

   a) are discussed   b) discussed
   c) be discussed

8 Why _____ about this problem?

   a) wasn't I told   b) was I told not
   c) I wasn't told

9 The money will _____ tomorrow.

   a) collect         b) to be collected
   c) be collected

10 The 1980s was my favourite _____.

   a) century         b) millennium     c) decade

11 We are making _____ all the time.

   a) movement        b) progress       c) advance

12 Lu _____ us directions to her house.

   a) did             b) gave           c) had

13 She was a very _____ musician.

   a) influencing     b) inspiration    c) influential

14 I have _____ what to do.

   a) a clue          b) no idea        c) ideas

15 I'm a hundred percent _____ of the answer.

   a) knowing         b) certainly      c) certain

16 We never eat _____ food.

   a) processed       b) process        c) reused

17 She said she _____ to talk to her boss.

   a) was going       b) going          c) would

18 You told me you _____ Bill for years.

   a) haven't to see  b) don't see      c) hadn't seen

19 He asked me when _____ in the country.

   a) I arrive        b) I'd arrived     c) I am arrive

20 She asked if we _____ how to get to Bristol.

   a) are knowing     b) did know       c) knew

21 I _____ the question.

   a) disunderstood   b) not understand
   c) misunderstood

22 I _____ to pay the bill, but she refused.

   a) offered         b) explained      c) invited

23 She _____ them that the water was dangerous.

   a) refused         b) warned         c) suggested

24 The man refused _____ me the gun.

   a) giving          b) for give       c) to give

25 The guide recommended _____ the museum.

   a) visiting        b) to visit       c) visit

26 My mother suggests _____ early as it gets crowded.

   a) that we are go  b) that we go     c) us to go

27 I warned you _____ that.

   a) not doing       b) not to do      c) to not do

28 I took it on the plane as hand _____.

   a) luggage         b) cases          c) bags

29 If I _____ pack some spare shoes.

   a) were you, you should
   b) were you, I'd
   c) am you, I'd

30 Please make _____ you sign your name.

   a) definite        b) sure           c) certainly

**TEST RESULT** | **/30**

# AUDIO SCRIPTS

**UNIT 1** Recording 1

1 What's your middle name?
2 Who gave you that?
3 Where's the best restaurant?
4 Why did they arrive late?
5 What did you have for lunch?
6 When does your train leave?

**UNIT 1** Recording 2

### Clyde

When I was growing up, my mother had this expression that she used all the time. She used to say, 'Keep your eyes open'. Very simple, I know, but she always said it. Like ... 'keep your eyes open' all the time. And so, well, we travelled quite a lot in those days, especially around Europe, and she always told us ... or encouraged us ... to look at different cultures and see the things around us. So in that respect, I think my mother really influenced me because now I appreciate other cultures and I do try to see the things around me.

### Luciana

Biggest influence? Well, my grandfather was definitely the biggest influence on me. I lived with my grandparents for about five years when I was a child, which is quite common in my country. And my grandfather was really strict. He was very tough. He was an immigrant who came from Italy with nothing, absolutely nothing, and he really believed in hard work. And everyone was frightened of him because he shouted a lot. But because I was his grand-daughter, I saw a different side of him. He could be very gentle, and quite a loving man. But his major thing was honesty. You had to tell the truth. He didn't mind if you made a mistake or did something wrong, but if you lied to him ... oh, he would get very, very angry. He made me an honest person and a hard-working person.

### Austin

I had an uncle – he's dead now – my Uncle Charlie. He was my mother's brother. And the thing about Charlie was that he was always happy. He always saw the bright side of life, which is something I've tried to do. He was a real character. He was built like a tank. I mean massive. I think he was some kind of boxing champion. And I remember him coming to our house at Christmas – this is when I was a kid – and laughing all the time. He had this big deep laugh. And he had a story that he always told us. He told it to us every Christmas, about a time in Australia when he fought a crocodile with his bare hands, basically killed this crocodile. And we believed every word of it. Many years later after he'd died, I asked my mother about this story and she looked at me funny and said, 'Your Uncle Charlie never went to Australia. He never left London in his whole life.'

**UNIT 1** Recording 3

1 He was an employee here.
2 I had a wonderful mentor.
3 All pupils wear a uniform.
4 We were team-mates for years.
5 Have you met my fiancée?
6 Talk to your partner.
7 She's my godmother.
8 That club is for members only.

**UNIT 2** Recording 1

1
A: Have you been here before?
B: Yes, we've visited Naples a few times.

2
A: Have you had time to see the museum yet?
B: No, we haven't had time.

3
A: Did you find your hotel OK?
B: Yes, we found the hotel without any problems.

4
A: Have you got your guidebook?
B: Oh no. I've left it in my room.

5
A: Have you had any lunch?
B: Yes, we've already eaten.

6
A: Have you enjoyed your stay?
B: Yes, we've had a wonderful time.

**UNIT 2** Recording 2

1
### Christine

A lot of friends were staying in my apartment. We'd had a party the night before, and in the morning, one friend, Danny, got up to make everyone some coffee. While he was making the coffee, he heard the news on the radio. He came back into the room, and told us that John Lennon had died. Someone had shot John Lennon. We were all really shocked. It was a very strange feeling. We couldn't believe it. We had all grown up with the music of John Lennon and The Beatles. We had played his music the night before. And now, suddenly, he waTs dead. There was a huge feeling of loss. He was such a peaceful man, who had wanted peace for everyone. It was a terrible way for him to die.

2
### Rob

I was travelling to a meeting on the Tube that morning, and there were delays everywhere. They closed the Underground station. At first, I was really angry, and worried about not getting to my meeting on time. But gradually, we started to realise that something terrible had happened. People outside the station were trying to talk on their mobile phones, but the networks were all down, because of the panic. Some people started to get news, and soon we discovered there had been bombs all over London. It was a strange and terrible feeling. There were crowds of people outside shops, watching the news on the televisions.

3
### Gino

I was sitting in the kitchen of my house in Italy with my family, and I was only a child. Everyone was watching television. I remember the black and white pictures. I watched as this man landed on the Moon. And I can remember thinking how amazing it must be to be an astronaut, and what an exciting job it was. Until then, I had wanted to be a train driver, but for a few years afterwards, I definitely wanted to be an astronaut.

**4**

**Marianne**

I was staying in Los Angeles with some friends, and I was only about eighteen years old. In the night I suddenly woke up, and the whole house was shaking. I had never felt an earthquake before, but I knew that was what was happening. It was very frightening. But after a few seconds it stopped, everything went quiet, and I went back to sleep. When I woke up in the morning, I thought perhaps it had all been a dream. But when I went downstairs, and turned on the radio, I heard the news. The quake was in San Francisco, and it had done a lot of damage. So, I was lucky really. But I will never forget that feeling.

## RC1 Recording 1

1 Who do you work for?
2 What type of things do you do?
3 What problems do you deal with?
4 When did you start working there?
5 Do you enjoy the job?
6 So why did you apply for this job?

## RC1 Recording 2

1 I've stopped.
2 We made it.
3 He helped me.
4 They've killed it.
5 You've worked hard.
6 I thanked her.

## UNIT 3 Recording 1

**Ruth**

I'm really excited about this weekend actually, because I'm ... I'm going walking with some friends in the Lake District. There's a whole group of us and we meet up every now and again for walking holidays. I love walking because it makes you feel so good, so we always have a good time. We're staying in a hostel, near one of the biggest lakes. There are some lovely walks from there and we've stayed in the hostel before. We're planning to do two big walks, one each day. They're about twenty- or thirty-kilometre walks, so it'll be quite hard, I think. We'll be really tired in the evenings, so we won't do much then, just have something to eat in the hostel, and then go to bed. It's not everyone's idea of fun, I know, but I can't wait.

**Kieron**

I'm starting at Dundee University in September. I'm going to study Law, so I'm really excited about it. I think it's going to be a good course, and I'm hoping to meet lots of new friends and have a good time, too. To start with, I'm going to stay in the university accommodation on campus, until I get to know the city better, and then I might move out and rent a flat with some other students. I'll have to see how it goes. Living on campus is cheaper, so I might stay there for the whole year. I'm planning to join a few clubs, probably the sports club, because I love sports. I enjoy playing rugby so I'll see if I can join the rugby club or something like that.

**Amber**

We're going to the Red Sea for our honeymoon, which is wonderful. I've never been to Egypt before, and I'm sure I'm going to love it. I love new experiences, meeting new people, and going to new places, and I think Egypt is going to feel really different. The language, the food, the way people behave, everything. We're staying in a luxury hotel right on the beach, and we're going to do a scuba-diving course while we're there. I've always wanted to try scuba-diving. It's going to be fantastic.

## UNIT 3 Recording 2

1 They're <u>going</u> to <u>play squash</u>.
2 I'm going to <u>buy</u> a new <u>phone</u>.
3 She's going to spend a <u>week</u> in <u>Greece</u>.
4 He <u>isn't</u> going to <u>eat</u> anything.
5 Are you <u>going</u> to <u>walk</u> to the <u>station</u>?
6 He's going to <u>change</u> his <u>job</u>.

## UNIT 3 Recording 3

1

**Conversation 1**

A: The living room is too green and the floor's all wrong.
B: Sorry?
A: The living room. Green. And I hate the floor.
B: You've lost me.
A: I'm talking about Mum's new house. I don't like the colour of the walls in the living room.
B: Oh!

**Conversation 2**

A: Hello? I'm trying to find my lost luggage.
B: Ah, OK.
A: My bags went missing in Montevideo in Uruguay, after a flight from Curitiba, Brazil.
B: Can you say that again? Montevideo?
A: I flew from Curitiba to Montevideo and my bags went missing.
B: Have you reported it already?
A: Yes, the name is Anders Kleeburg.
B: Hang on. Could you repeat the last name? Anders ...?
A: Kleeburg. K-l-e-e-b-u-r-g.

**Conversation 3**

A: OK, so cricket. So this is the bowler, OK? He runs up and bowls at the batsman.
B: What exactly do you mean? What's a bowler?
A: A bowler is the person with the ball in his hand, OK? And he tries to get the batsman out. Get him off the field.
B: Do you mean to say he tries to kill the batsman with the ball?
A: No!

**Conversation 4**

A: Did you read this?! About popcorn. In 1948, two American scientists found some popcorn in a cave in New Mexico and dated it. It was over five thousand years old.
B: I didn't catch any of that. Are you talking about popcorn?
A: Yeah, it's an ancient food. Popcorn is thousands of years old.
B: I don't get what you're saying. You mean the popcorn we ate in the cinema yesterday is thousands of years old!
A: No! Popcorn in general. People have eaten it for thousands of years.

## UNIT 4  Recording 1

**1**

I work in a busy airport in France. I am responsible for a small group of people. In my job you need to know what you are doing. You must be very accurate, and observant. And you have to be able to work well under pressure and be a good decision maker.

**2**

I work in a pizza restaurant. In my job you need to have a friendly, relaxed manner. It's important to be friendly to customers, and patient. You have to be organised, and have a good memory, too.

**3**

In my job you have to be a really good communicator. You need to be able to listen carefully to customers, and find out what the problem is. And then you have to be able to think outside the box sometimes to see if you can find a solution to the problem, which will keep everybody happy. You have to be able to stay calm, even if the customer starts getting angry.

**4**

I work in a lawyer's office. You have to have good organisational skills, I think, and you shouldn't get stressed too easily. You have to be quite hard-working as well. And you need to pay attention to detail.

**5**

I work in a children's hospital. I think the most important quality for my job is that you must be a caring person. You have to care about the people you're looking after. And you have to get on with children. That's very important.

**6**

You need to be very patient in my job, especially when there's a lot of traffic. And you have to be a good timekeeper as well. You always have to be on time.

## UNIT 4  Recording 2

1  I used to be very sporty.
2  Can I use your phone?
3  He never used to worry about it.
4  I used to live in the USA when I was 18.
5  This stuff is used to kill insects.
6  I don't use the car much any more.
7  We used to love going there on holiday.
8  I didn't use to live in Europe.

## RC 2  Recording 1

amazing
successful
delicious
exhausted
salary
interview
furious
difficult
tasty
leader
boiling
freezing
competitive
impossible

## UNIT 5  Recording 1

/eɪ/ **make**
space
communications
aeroplanes
vaccinations

/æ/ **apple**
antibiotics
travel
satellites
vacuum

/ə/ **polar**
nuclear
machine
commercial
solar

## UNIT 5  Recording 2

**Mia**

Well, it's changed a lot, goodness, enormously. I mean thirty years ago, I was still at school. I was ten years old. Life was a lot simpler then. All I had to think about was doing my homework, and enjoying my free time with friends. I think life was simpler for everybody then. We didn't have all this technology, and I think the pace of life was slower. At work, when someone sent a letter, it could take a week or two even before they would get a reply. Nowadays, people email, and they expect an instant response. On the same day, or within an hour or two. That puts a lot of pressure on people. We say that technology has saved us time, but it just speeds things up, and we are expected to do so much more. It's non-stop. We have mobile phones and BlackBerries, iPhones. So we don't just turn off and relax.

**Tom**

That's an interesting question. It's changed a lot. I live in Beijing. So there has been a huge advancement of technology, and huge growth. There are more people, with more money. There has been an economic explosion here, so the city has grown. All the offices and high-rise buildings, lots of those weren't here thirty years ago. And it's very multicultural nowadays. People from all over the world live in Beijing. People came from everywhere to see if they could get rich, and many of them did get rich. They made millions. I think in a lot of places out in the countryside, things haven't changed that much. Life is quite similar to how it was before, for farmers, and their families. I suppose they have more technology now. They have mobile phones, and televisions, and the internet, so they know a lot more about the wider world, and what is going on. Thirty years ago, they just had a radio, and it was difficult to find out information. That's much easier now.

**Owen**

Oh, well, both probably. The world is getting better in many ways. I think if we look at living standards across the world, obviously there are still millions of people living in terrible poverty, but I think the situation is getting better. People have better access to food and medicines, and education. So, these are all things which are improving. Medicine is improving, so people live longer, and we can fight infectious diseases. People's lives have improved because of technology, so life is easier now than it was before. A lot of manual work is done by machines. But in some ways, the world is getting worse. War, for example, is a bigger problem all the time. There are more and more wars, which is surprising. And weapons are becoming even more dangerous. I think the environment is definitely suffering, so we are polluting more than we used to because of all the industrialisation. And I think also, socially, things are getting worse. Because people are less social now, than before. They spend more time on their own, with computers and computer games, and less time talking to others, working together, and I think that is a great shame, and a problem for the future, too.

## UNIT 5 Recording 3

**1**
A: Have you met Yinka's parents?
B: Only once. They're doctors, aren't they?

**2**
A: There isn't a cloud in the sky.
B: I know. It's a beautiful day, isn't it?

**3**
A: Are you looking for the scissors?
B: You haven't seen them, have you?

**4**
A: Have you read Jhumpa Lahiri's new book?
B: Yeah, she's a great writer, isn't she?

**5**
A: I've got my final exam tomorrow.
B: You'll pass, won't you?

**6**
A: I think this is the wrong address.
B: Yes, we've made a mistake, haven't we?

## UNIT 5 Recording 4

**1**
A: Excuse me, could you tell me the way to the swimming pool, please?
B: Yes, of course I can. You keep going this way, until you get to the traffic lights. Then, …

**2**
A: Hello. Do you know what time the bank opens?
B: I'm not sure. I'll just ask someone.

**3**
A: Do you want us to bring anything?
B: That would be great. Could you bring some salad, and maybe something for dessert?
A: Yes, of course. Anything else?
B: No, that'll be fine.

**4**
A: Could you help me with my bags?
B: I'm sorry, I can't. I've got my hands full.

**5**
A: Would you mind opening the door for me?
B: Of course not. There you are.
A: Thank you. That's very kind.

**6**
A: Could you tell me what time the show starts?
B: Let me have a look. The afternoon show starts at 3p.m.
A: Thanks very much.

**7**
A: Would you mind coming to get me from the station?
B: OK. Sure. Wait outside and I'll be there in ten minutes.

**8**
A: Do you know if there's a post office near here?
B: Yes, there is – there's one just along this road.

## UNIT 6 Recording 1

1 If I had more time, I'd learn to ski.
2 If you didn't work, what would you do?
3 If they had to move, they wouldn't live with me.
4 She'd go out at night if her parents let her.
5 Where would you go if you had the chance?
6 I wouldn't sleep if I drank that coffee.

## UNIT 6 Recording 2

In the eyes of street criminals, everybody communicates something. Some people communicate strength and power; others communicate 'I am a victim'. Researchers Jean A Hampton and Robert Ealey asked convicted criminals to watch a secret video of a street scene and then say which people look like possible victims of a crime. They did it easily. The potential victims, surprisingly, were not always small women; sometimes they were big men. For this interview, Robert Ealey looked at this picture of a street scene and explained which people were potential victims.

## UNIT 6 Recording 3

I = Interviewer  E = Robert Ealey

I: So which of these people would a criminal go for?
E: Not the ones you think.
I: Can you explain?
E: Yeah, so for example, you've got an old woman, see?
I: Yes.
E: So you're a criminal, OK? You might think, OK, this old woman is small and weak. She's not going to fight me or give me any trouble. But who's she with?
I: She's with a dog.
E: That's right. And the thing about dogs is they are unpredictable. And the last thing you want if you're a criminal is unpredictability. You have about five seconds maximum to commit the crime and you don't want any surprises. OK? So you leave the old woman.
I: Right. Is that really the length of time for a street crime?
E: Five seconds? That's the maximum. Most street crimes take maybe two seconds, then it's over.
I: Wow.
E: OK, so let's take someone else. There's a woman talking into a mobile phone, OK?
I: Yes, I see her.
E: Easy victim or not?
I: Well, if she's talking on a mobile phone, she could tell her friend what's happening, right?
E: And then what?
I: Um, the friend calls the police?
E: And do you think the police are going to get there in five seconds?
I: Well, no.
E: No, this woman on the phone is a potential victim. The phone doesn't matter. The reason she's a potential victim is that she isn't paying attention to what's happening around her. She isn't looking at other people. She's distracted.
I: I see.
E: The same with the tourists looking at the map, OK?
I: Right.
E: They're concentrating on the map, not the people around them. This also tells the criminal that these people are lost and don't know what they're doing.
I: But there are two of them, right, so maybe a criminal would hesitate?
E: Maybe, but don't forget, it takes half a second to steal something and run. OK, what about the man at the cashpoint?
I: The guy taking cash out of the bank?
E: What's he doing wrong?
I: Well, if that was me, the cash would be in my wallet before I turned round.
E: That's right. He's basically saying, 'look at me, I've just taken out lots of money and I'm too stupid to put it in my wallet quickly'. He's a criminal's dream. What about the woman in a mini-skirt?
I: Well, she's attractive and … I don't know. She's not exactly big and strong either. Maybe a victim?
E: But look at her body language. She's confident, she knows where she's going, she's looking straight ahead, and she's probably moving fast. No criminal would go for her.
I: That's interesting. So body language is pretty important.
E: It's extremely important. Look at the man in the coat. Big man, probably strong, but what's his body telling us?
I: He's not focusing.

E: Yes, that's right. He's looking at his feet. He doesn't know who's around him. Any criminal will think, 'nice coat, probably a fat wallet in there, full of money, and he's not concentrating'. The key for a street criminal is surprise. It doesn't matter who the victim is; if you can surprise them, they have no chance.

I: The couple leaving the taxi?

E: Rule number one of the street: if you have anything valuable, don't show it. This man's wearing an expensive watch which everyone can see. The other thing is people leaving cars are always in a weak position. They aren't standing up properly, and they aren't aware of who else is on the street.

## UNIT 6 Recording 4

**Conversation 1**

A: Bad news, I'm afraid.
B: What's the matter?
A: I'm afraid it needs a new engine.

**Conversation 2**

A: What's the problem?
B: I'm sorry to have to tell you, but we lost the match.

**Conversation 3**

A: I've got some good news for you.
B: What's that?
A: We've won a holiday for two in Turkey!

**Conversation 4**

A: I'm afraid I've got some bad news.
B: What's happened?
A: The flight's been cancelled.

**Conversation 5**

A: There's something I've got to tell you.
B: What's that?
A: I failed my exam.

**Conversation 6**

A: You'll never guess what happened.
B: What?
A: I was promoted!

**Conversation 7**

A: Unfortunately, we were burgled last night.
B: Oh no. That's terrible.

**Conversation 8**

A: I've got something to tell you.
B: What is it?
A: We're getting married.

## UNIT 7 Recording 1

**1**
He's very gifted.
She's really skilful.

**2**
He has an aptitude.
I'm hopeless at this.

**3**
He thinks he's useless.
She has a talent.

**4**
They say he's an expert.
She has great ability.

## UNIT 7 Recording 2

A: Sidis was the greatest genius in history.
B: William Sidis? A genius.
C: Probably the greatest mind of the twentieth century.
D: They say his IQ was between two hundred and fifty and three hundred. That's off the scale.
E: A genius.
F: William Sidis? Great brain, difficult life.
G: Sidis? Genius.

Was William Sidis the most intelligent man who ever lived? If so, why isn't he famous? Why isn't his name known like the names of Einstein, Leonardo, and Charles Darwin? What can his life teach us?

William James Sidis was born on April 1st in 1898. That's right: April the first, April Fool's Day. His parents were Boris and Sarah Sidis, Russian-Jewish immigrants who had settled in New York. They were both passionately interested in education. Boris was a psychologist who taught at Harvard University and Sarah used to read Greek myths to her son as bedtime stories.

It soon became clear that their son was something special. Aged six months, William said his first word: '**door**'. At seven months, he pointed at the moon and said 'Moon'. At eighteen months, William could read *The New York Times*. And aged three, he reached up to a typewriter and wrote a letter to a shop called Macy's, asking them to send him some toys! At six, he could speak Russian, French, German and Hebrew.

All of this took place at home, but soon he made newspaper headlines. He passed the entrance exam to one of the United States' best universities at the age of eight. Then, aged nine, he gave a lecture on mathematics at Harvard University. Attended by maths professors and graduate students, this lecture put Sidis on the map. He began attending Harvard University two years later, at the age of eleven.

Now that he was in the public eye, things began to go wrong for William Sidis. The media was fascinated by him. Journalists followed him around and wrote articles about this young genius. Not surprisingly, Sidis began to feel like an animal in a zoo, with everyone watching him.

He wasn't interested in becoming famous, nor in becoming an academic. He just wanted to live a quiet, private life. He tried. He went from job to job, publishing only one book of any academic interest. But everywhere he went, whatever he did, people eventually learned who he was, and the press kept writing about him. In 1944, he died aged 46, almost forgotten.

Since his death, many stories have been told about Sidis. Some said that his genius burned out like an old light bulb. His sister said Sidis knew all the languages of the world and that he could learn a language in a day. None of this was true. Even his IQ – which was supposed to be between 250 and 300 – was just a guess. No intelligence test has been invented to go to that level of genius.

So what can we learn from his life? Firstly, not all childhood geniuses will produce great things as adults. They may think great thoughts or do incredible calculations, but many of them just do normal jobs and find happiness in that way. Secondly, Sidis spent much of his time and energy running away from fame. Unless they want to be Hollywood stars, people need to be left in peace. That's how most geniuses do great work.

## UNIT 7 Recording 3

### Conversation 1

A: We really need to stop this. In my view, it's getting out of control. For example, she watched TV for six hours yesterday. Six hours!

B: I must say that's a lot.

A: It *is* a lot. She needs to get out more.

B: And when she's not in front of the TV, she's on the internet.

A: That's what I was saying. She's always in front of a screen.

### Conversation 2

A: For me, Elizabeth is the best. She would be really good in this job.

B: Why do you think so?

A: For one thing, she has the right qualifications. For another, she obviously really wants the job.

B: Yeah, that's very clear. I think the other woman …

A: Hayla.

B: Hayla. She would do a good job, too.

A: She would, but having said that, she already has a good job. You can see that Elizabeth is really hungry for this position.

### Conversation 3

A= Presenter   B = Mr Dyson

A: Mr Dyson, in your presentation you said that the arts in many schools weren't getting enough attention. Can you explain?

B: Yes, the reason I say this is that funding has been cut for arts subjects. There just isn't enough money. Let me give you an example. A school I visited last month wanted to do a play in the little school theatre, but there was no money for costumes, for music. So in the end there was no school play, and the theatre was closed for the whole summer term.

A: And this is a money issue?

B: I do think we could solve a lot of the problems if the government recognised the arts as it recognises maths or science or reading, yes. Like I said, money isn't everything, but it's part of the problem.

## UNIT 8 Recording 1

### Elise

E = Elise   I = Interviewer

E: I live next door to my parents, who are on one side, and my brother's family, who are on the other side.

I: Right.

E: It's really, really useful. They're the perfect neighbours.

I: In what sense?

E: Well, I like the situation because we help each other. For example, if I need a babysitter for my kids, it's no problem.

I: And you see each other a lot?

E: We work together in the family business so we see each other every day. And I guess the whole extended family, which is eleven of us including the children, we eat together maybe once or twice a week, always on Sundays and sometimes during the week. So, yes, we do see each other a lot.

I: You never get fed up with the family?

E: No, I think this situation is quite normal in a lot of countries, maybe like Italy. It certainly is for our family. We've always lived in the same town. I've lived here all my life, and we always wanted to live side by side. I hope our children continue the business and live here, too.

I: And what about your husband? Does he like being so close to your family?

E: Um, I've never asked him actually! Yeah, course he does! I think.

### Marc

M = Marc   I = Interviewer

M: We don't have any neighbours. Our nearest neighbours are a couple of cows that live in a field about ten miles away.

I: Are they good neighbours?

M: Fantastic! Very quiet! No, we really are completely isolated.

I: So how come? I mean, was this your dream?

M: Well, it wasn't at first. We were living in Paris, which is a great city, but it's kind of big and we got tired of crowds of people, and all the noise and using public transport. So about ten years ago, we bought an old farmhouse in the middle of nowhere. It's not a functioning farm, but it has an internet connection and me and my wife both work online. And we just love the peace and quiet.

I: So the cows aren't yours?

M: No, they belong to a farmer about ten miles away!

I: And isn't it a bit lonely out here?

M: We love it. We never see our neighbours, apart from the cows, which is just fantastic for us as we're a bit antisocial. Actually, you're the first person we've seen this year!

I: Oh, sorry to interrupt your peace!

M: Not a problem. Just don't stay too long!

## UNIT 8 Recording 2

1 traffic lights
2 high street
3 housing estate
4 sports centre
5 industrial estate
6 car park
7 supermarket
8 language school
9 shopping centre
10 one-way street
11 terraced houses
12 outdoor market
13 gift shop
14 primary school

## UNIT 8 Recording 3

1 The website which we built is too slow.

2 Those people who are always working don't enjoy life.

3 The ratings site, which I check every day, is growing fast.

4 Those students who do online courses love studying.

5 Near my flat, where you're staying, there's a supermarket.

## UNIT 9 Recording 1

1  If I'd known you were coming, I would've waited.
2  If I'd waited, I would've been late.
3  If I'd been late, I would've missed the show.
4  If I'd missed the show, I would've wasted my money.
5  If I'd wasted my money, I would've been angry.

## UNIT 9 Recording 2

Hello, and welcome to 'Fascinating Facts!' Today we're going to take a look at some those 'modern' inventions which turn out to be … well, not quite so modern at all!

Let's start with toothpaste. So you think, 'hmm, toothpaste – when was that invented?' A hundred years ago? Maybe two hundred? But we find that actually, toothpaste has been around for sixteen hundred years. People from Egypt used it, and then the Ancient Greeks and Romans used it. Was it the same as modern toothpaste? Definitely not. Ancient Greek toothpaste used ingredients like crushed bones and oyster shells.

OK, another invention for you: biological weapons. Again, you think, 'biological weapons – must be a twentieth-century invention'. Wrong again. Biological weapons have been used for over three thousand years. Probably beginning in Ancient Greece, it was common for one side to poison their enemy's water supply during a war. Some generals would even throw dead bodies at the enemy or into the enemy's river. One leader called Hannibal even put poisonous snakes into pots and threw them onto an enemy's ship. In the eighteenth century, one way American Indians were killed was through using infected blankets given to them by the Europeans who were colonising America.

Next topic: football. Just how old is the game? The answer is, we don't really know. But we do know that forms of it were played in China over two thousand years ago. And it also seems that the game developed by chance in different parts of the world. Wherever European explorers went, they discovered that native people already played some kind of football: Aborigines in Australia, the Inuit in Greenland, Japan and the Americas. So I suppose it really is the people's game.

Right. Central heating. It's been a wonderful thing for us in cold countries and helps us get through the winters.

But most of us don't realise it's a very old invention. Once again, the Ancient Greeks were the first in Europe, over two thousand years ago, although there was a similar system in Korea. Both of these civilisations had pipes and controlled fires under the floors to keep the buildings warm. In England, one of the first examples of central heating was in the 1830s. A rich banker installed it in his house so that he could grow grapes in England's cold weather!

The final invention we're going to look at today is the good old umbrella. If we look at a number of ancient sculptures from Egypt and Persia, which is now called Iran, it's clear that the umbrella has been around for a long, long time, certainly more than two thousand years. Interestingly, it seems that only kings or very important people had umbrellas in these sculptures. So they were a symbol of high social class. But what were they for? In Europe we tend to think of umbrellas as things to protect us from the rain. But historically, they protected people from the sun. And later, they became a fashion item.

## UNIT 9 Recording 3

1  The Institute is given almost a million euros a year.
2  One day a cure for cancer will be discovered.
3  The files were stolen last year.
4  These famous photos were taken at the end of the war.
5  The President hasn't been told about the plan.
6  The missing people have been found.
7  All flights going out of Paris were cancelled.
8  The paintings are cleaned once a year.

## UNIT 9 Recording 4

1
A: Marisa had her baby yesterday.
B: Did she? What wonderful news!

2
A: I'm doing an online project about Second Life.
B: Oh really? That's interesting.

3
A: His cousin was an Olympic boxer.
B: Was he? Wow!

4
A: My sister doesn't eat meat.
B: Doesn't she? OK, I'll cook fish.

5
A: The King of Italy? There isn't one! Italy is a republic.
B: I was just about to say that.

6
A: I love Lady Gaga!
B: Do you? I think she's crazy.

7
A: The inventor of the internet? It was Tim Berners-Lee.
B: Oh yes, I knew that. I just couldn't remember.

8
A: My parents have never been here.
B: Haven't they? When are they going to visit?

9
A: Jake was the number one student in the country.
B: Really? I didn't know that.

10
A: John's got the car. We'll have to travel by bus.
B: Will we? Oh, that's annoying.

## UNIT 10 Recording 1

P = Presenter   A = Amy   J = Jay-Jay
P: In 2007, one city decided to take a stand against climate change. Two point two million people across Sydney switched off their lights for an event that would become known across the world as Earth Hour. Earth Hour quickly went global, spreading across the world, and in 2010, thousands of cities in 128 countries took part. Global landmarks like the Eiffel Tower in Paris, the Egyptian Pyramids, New York's Empire State Building, and Sydney Harbour Bridge all plunged into darkness, as millions of people around the world switched their lights off to protest against climate change.

Organisers say that they want to demonstrate what people can do to reduce their carbon footprint and save energy, and thus draw attention to the problem of climate change. However, critics describe the event as meaningless. In today's programme, we're asking what you think. Can Earth Hour really make a difference? Is it a good way to raise awareness about the problems the world is facing? Have you taken part in the switch-off? First on the line, we have Amy. Amy, can you tell us what you think?

A: I think Earth Hour is a great idea. It's a really simple way for people to show that they care about the environment, and want something to change.

P: So, did you do anything for Earth Hour last year, Amy?

A: Yes, I did. I was at home with my two children, who are eight and thirteen years old, and we switched the lights off at home, and had our dinner by candlelight.

P: And how did you find that? What did the children think?

A: It was brilliant. The children loved it, and we enjoyed a really quiet hour, with no television, or music. We talked, actually. And we'll be doing it again this year, definitely.

P: Thank you, Amy. Thanks for calling. Now, we've got Jay-Jay on the line. Jay-Jay, what do you think of Earth Hour?

J: I think it's a complete waste of time. I can't believe it.

P: Wow. And why is that, Jay-Jay? What's the problem?

J: I don't understand how anybody can think that turning off your lights for one hour is really going to make any difference. It's just a way for people to do something which makes them feel better. They turn their lights off for an hour, and then they think they have done something about climate change. And then they can carry on as they were before. What we need is for people to really change how they behave, every day, not just for an hour. They need to use less electricity, not drive around in their cars everywhere. We need governments to make big changes, and turning your lights off ... well, it's just silly.

P: But don't you think, Jay-Jay, that it is a symbol, a gesture that helps to get people around the world thinking about the problems?

J: Yes, you're right. But the main problem is not to get people thinking about it, but to get people to actually change the way that they live, and that's not easy.

P: You're right about that. I suppose ...

## UNIT 10 Recording 2

1 Gina refused to come with us.
2 He promised to call me later.
3 They decided to go out for a meal.
4 They agreed not to go on holiday this year.
5 She warned us that the restaurant was very expensive.
6 They invited James to go to the theatre with them on Friday.
7 The teacher explained that the children grow vegetables in the garden.
8 He recommended buying our fruit at the market.

# ANSWER KEY

## UNIT 1

### 1.1

#### 1A
2 great-grandparents
3 family history
4 related to
5 relatives
6 ancestors
7 inherited
8 side of the family
9 roots
10 takes after

#### B
1 roots
2 extended
3 family history
4 great
5 side
6 relatives
7 ancestors
8 related to

#### 2A
2 b 3 a 4 b 5 b 6 a 7 a 8 b

#### B
b 6 c 8 d 1 e 7 f 4 g 3 h 5

#### 3
1 c 2 a 3 a 4 c 5 b 6 c

#### 4A
1 What's your middle name?
2 Who gave you that?
3 Where's the best restaurant?
4 Why did they arrive late?
5 What did you have for lunch?
6 When does your train leave?

#### 5A
**Clyde**
Who? His mother
How? She encouraged him to 'keep his eyes open' – to look at different cultures and see things around him.
**Luciana**
Who? Her grandfather
How? He made her an honest and hard-working person.
**Austin**
Who? Uncle Charlie
How? He was always happy. He always saw the bright side of life.

#### B
1 Keep your eyes open.
2 He travelled around Europe.
3 For about five years.
4 honesty
5 In Australia he fought and killed a crocodile with his bare hands.
6 He never went to Australia and never left London.

#### C
1 d 2 a 3 f 4 e 5 b 6 c

#### 6A
Email 2 needs to be formal.

#### B
1 Hi Pilar
2 How are you?
3 thought I'd
4 really like
5 can't wait to stay
6 Hope
7 Dear members
8 I am writing to introduce myself
9 I would like to take this opportunity
10 I will explain
11 I look forward to working with you all
12 Yours sincerely

### 1.2

#### 1
1 are, found
2 won, was sleeping
3 don't like, didn't … tell
4 Did … hear, were driving
5 Do … need, 'm staying
6 'm reading, didn't finish
7 get up, leave
8 're waiting, was looking

#### 2
2 a ii, b i
3 a i, b ii
4 a ii, b i
5 a ii, b i

#### 3A
1 employee, boss
2 classmate, pupil
3 fiancée, fiancé, godfather, godmother
4 team-mate, member

#### B
1 fiancée 2 classmate 3 boss
4 member 5 pupil 6 employee
7 godfather 8 team-mate

#### 4A
1 employ<u>ee</u> 2 <u>men</u>tor 3 <u>pu</u>pils
4 <u>team</u>-mates 5 fi<u>an</u>cée 6 <u>part</u>ner
7 <u>god</u>mother 8 <u>mem</u>bers

#### 5A
1 men – said by women
2 men – said by women
3 women – said by women
4 women – said by women

#### C
2 Mai 3 Guy 4 Sergio 5 Linda 6 Avril

#### D
1 spatial perception 2 equip 3 further
4 distantly 5 instincts

#### 6A
2 go 3 take 4 do 5 do 6 get 7 go
8 do 9 take 10 get 11 take 12 go

### 1.3

#### 1A
1 d 2 g 3 e 4 h 5 f 6 c 7 b 8 a

#### 2A
**Conversation 1**
Could I ask a question?
In my opinion
**Conversation 2**
There are a couple of things I'd like to ask about.
For me, the most important thing
**Conversation 3**
I have a query.
One thing I'd like to say is that
**Conversation 4**
Can I ask you about that?
I'd have to say 'yes'.

#### B
A 4 B 1 C 2 D 3

#### 3
1 a 2 b 3 c 4 c 5 a 6 a 7 a 8 c
9 c 10 b

## UNIT 2

### 2.1

#### 1A
1 action
2 biopic
3 fantasy
4 period drama

5 romantic comedy

6 adventure

7 disaster

8 crime, thriller, comedy

9 docudrama

**B**

1 biopic

2 disaster

3 romantic comedy

4 fantasy

5 action / thriller

6 crime

**2A**

1 've never been, went

2 have you acted, 've acted

3 has travelled, has he visited

4 has won, won

5 lived, did they move

6 Have you been, arrived

7 've been married, met

8 Did you enjoy, haven't had

**3**

2 's / has been

3 've / have worked

4 've / have lived in

5 haven't seen Robbie

6 've / have been to London

**4A**

1 we've visited

2 we haven't had

3 we found

4 've left

5 we've already

6 we've had

**5**

1 at  2 in  3 on  4 at  5 on  6 In  7 by  8 in
9 in  10 by  11 on  12 on

**6A/B**

1 T

2 F (He was twenty-four years old.)

3 F (He wasn't speeding at the time of the accident.)

4 F (He had a motorcycle accident and lost two teeth.)

5 F (His favourite drink was coffee.)

**C**

1 b  2 c  3 a  4 c

**D**

1 barely out of their teens

2 immortalised

3 rebellious attitude

4 a lasting impression

5 assumed

## 2.2

**1A**

1 T  2 F

**B**

A 3  B 4  C 1  D 2

**C**

1 Rob

2 Gino

3 Danny, a friend

4 people outside the station

5 Marianne

6 John Lennon

**2**

1 b  2 a  3 a  4 b  5 a  6 a

**3**

1 happened

2 waited

3 didn't come

4 was driving

5 broke

6 had run out

7 Did … enjoy

8 hated

9 had booked

10 hadn't realised / didn't realise

11 were coming

12 was pouring

13 spilled

14 ordered

15 had said / said

16 arrived

17 tasted

**4A**

1 crash  2 earthquake  3 hostages
4 floods  5 fugitive  6 demonstration
7 shot  8 attacked  9 collapse  10 strikes

**B**

1 a  2 b  3 b  4 a  5 a

**5A**

**Report A**

a 2  b 3  c 1

**Report B**

a 3  b 2  c 1

**Report C**

a 3  b 2  c 1

**B**

**Report A**

1 A priest installed an electronic fingerprint reader in his church.

2 Warsaw, Poland

3 They want to monitor whether the children attend mass or not.

**Report B**

1 There was a 'Love Message Yelling Event'.

2 Hibiya Park in central Tokyo, Japan

3 Kiyotaka Yamana started the event after his own marriage failed, to encourage people to be more romantic.

**Report C**

1 More than 1,000 tourists had to be evacuated from Machu Picchu in helicopters.

2 Machu Picchu, Peru

3 The ruins had been cut off by floods and mudslides.

**C**

1 as soon as  2 During  3 While  4 Until
5 During  6 by the time  7 until

## 2.3

**1**

1 told  2 say  3 told  4 told  5 say  6 said

**2**

1 This happened when

2 Well

3 so

4 Anyway

5 Before long

6 The next thing I knew

7 In the end

8 Anyway

**3**

1 happened  2 no  3 kidding  4 what
5 then  6 Oh  7 Really  8 amazing

## REVIEW AND CHECK 1

**1**

1 related  2 side  3 after  4 extended
5 relatives  6 inherited  7 grandparents
8 roots

**2A**

1 do you work for

2 do you do

3 do you deal with

4 did you start

5 Do you enjoy

6 did you apply

**3**

| | |
|---|---|
| 1 'm | 6 was looking |
| 2 'm taking | 7 was reading |
| 3 didn't start | 8 jumped |
| 4 love | 9 isn't |
| 5 saw | 10 wanted |

## 4A/B

1 <u>boss</u>
2 <u>class</u>mate
3 <u>team</u>-mate
4 <u>men</u>tor
5 fi<u>an</u>cée
6 emplo<u>yee</u>
7 <u>pu</u>pil
8 <u>part</u>ner

## 5

2 took, took
3 did, went
4 do, take
5 take, go
6 went, got

## 6

1 c 2 b 3 a 4 c 5 a 6 c

## 7

3 but 4 ✔ 5 am 6 ✔ 7 to 8 It's 9 ✔
10 really 11 the (my opinion) 12 for
13 ✔ 14 ✔

## 8

1 You're welcome.
2 No problem.
3 Of course.
4 You're correct.
5 Go ahead.
6 I see.
7 That's right.
8 I understand.
9 Please continue.

## 9

1 biopic, strike
2 thriller, fugitive
3 comedy, crash
4 science, attack
5 fantasy, earthquake
6 period, collapse
7 action, shot

## 10

1 fell
4 Did you go
7 didn't sell

## 11

1 b 2 a 3 a 4 b 5 b 6 a

## 12

1 for 2 by 3 in 4 on 5 on 6 at 7 on
8 in 9 in 10 on 11 by 12 By 13 on
14 by 15 in

## 13

1 stayed
2 had left
3 was listening
4 was wearing
5 hadn't turned on
6 didn't finish
7 hadn't been
8 opened
9 were doing
10 didn't eat

## 14A

1 tell 2 say 3 tell 4 say 5 tell 6 say

## B

1 told stories
2 tell jokes
3 said sorry
4 says 'hello'
5 told a white lie
6 say what you mean

## 15

1 This happened
2 happened
3 Anyway
4 In
5 Oh no
6 Well
7 before
8 So
9 did you do
10 Finally
11 The next thing
12 Oh dear
13 a sudden
14 happened then
15 in
16 funny

## TEST

1 a 2 c 3 c 4 a 5 b 6 a 7 b 8 c 9 c
10 b 11 a 12 c 13 c 14 a 15 b 16 b
17 c 18 b 19 a 20 b 21 a 22 c 23 b
24 c 25 c 26 a 27 c 28 b 29 c 30 b

## UNIT 3

### 3.1

**1A**
a Kieron b Amber c Ruth

**B**
1 b 2 b 3 c 4 b 5 b 6 c 7 a 8 c 9 a

**C**
1 e 2 d 3 a 4 b 5 c

## 2

1 b 2 a 3 a 4 b 5 a 6 a 7 b 8 a

## 3

1 Are you doing
2 are going out
3 might try / are going to try
4 're / are meeting / 're / are going to
   meet
5 'll / will be
6 're / are going to be
7 is playing
8 might go
9 'll / will call

## 4A

1 a 2 b 3 b 4 b 5 a 6 b

## 5

**Across**
3 chat 5 boast 6 compliment 8 warn
**Down**
1 gossip 2 apologise 4 argue 7 moan

## 6A

1 d 2 c 3 f 4 b 5 a 6 e

## B

1 **I've** gone to lunch. **I'll be** back soon.
2 Mr Jackson called (**earlier**). **He didn't
   leave a** message. (**He said that**) **He**
   will call again later.
3 **My** dentist appointment **has been**
   cancelled. I need to rebook.
4 **I'm** at the cinema. **Your** dinner **is** in the
   oven. **I'll** see you later.
5 **I'm** going (**to go**) swimming after
   school – **do you** want to come (**with
   me**)?
6 **I'm** sorry, I didn't tidy **my** bedroom –
   I was late for school.

## 3.2

**1**
b

**2**
1 To communicate with extraterrestrial
   life.
2 hello
3 SETI sends signals into space.
4 150 full-time scientists, educators and
   other staff.
5 For three or four decades.
6 They think that secret government
   agencies are examining crashed UFOs
   and the bodies of dead aliens.

**3**
1 e 2 d 3 a 4 c 5 b

**4**
1 radio waves 2 enslave 3 species
4 bunker

## 5A

2 future  3 term  4 short  5 in  6 from
7 time  8 next

## B

1, 2, 4, 5 and 8 are about things that will happen soon.

3, 6 and 7 are about things that will happen more than three years in the future.

## 6

2 will you stay
3 you going to speak to Ted tomorrow
4 is unlikely to pass her exam
5 going to be a storm
6 could become the champion
7 are likely to find a cure for cancer one day
8 may not be able to attend the meeting
9 won't have time to go shopping
10 could meet next week

## 7

1 are  2 be  3 won't  4 to  5 to
6 be / become  7 will  8 are

## 8

2 foot  3 tea  4 rat  5 eye  6 working
7 run  8 piece  9 hot  10 mind  11 hand

## 3.3

### 1

A 4  B 3  C 1  D 2

### 2

1 lost  2 Can  3 again  4 repeat  5 What
6 mean  7 say  8 catch  9 get  10 saying

### 3

1 So you're saying we can't come in.
2 Didn't you say it starts at ten o'clock?
3 So what you mean is we failed.
4 Do you mean to tell me that it costs €50,000?
5 In other words, we are the champions.

## UNIT 4

## 4.1

### 1A

1 good communicator
2 hard-working
3 lazy
4 ambitious
5 good leader
6 competitive
7 indecisive
8 outside the box
9 motivated
10 risk taker

## B

2 competitive
3 hard-working
4 motivated
5 good communicator
6 good leader
7 risk taker
8 ambitious

## 2

1 e  don't have to
2 i  shouldn't
3 b  should
4 g  mustn't
5 a  should
6 j  have to
7 d  mustn't
8 h  must
9 c  don't have to
10 f  must

## 3

2 I've finished this exercise. What ~~I should~~ **should I** do now?
3 The clients don't ~~has~~ **have** to come to the office. We can meet them at the restaurant.
4 I shouldn't ~~to~~ tell you this, but the boss is leaving on Monday.
5 Do we have **to** wear a uniform?
6 Everybody must ~~leaving~~ **leave** the building by 6p.m.
7 She ~~have~~ **has** to be at work by 7.30a.m.
8 I think you should ~~to~~ check what time the film starts.
9 You ~~don't must~~ **mustn't** use a mobile phone in the classroom.
10 We have **to** wait until the IT man comes to fix the system.

## 4B

A 3  B 1  C 6  D 5  E 4  F 2

## C

1 2
2 4
3 4
4 5
5 6
6 1
7 1
8 3

## 5A

1 listen, leave
2 remind, remember
3 fun
4 job, earn
5 work, forget
6 hear, won, funny

## B

1 remind
2 hear, won
3 job
4 forget
5 work, fun
6 funny

## 4.2

## B

1 good salary, beachside mansion, fantastic views of the ocean
2 Because Ben was too busy, and there wasn't much time to relax.
3 He was stung by a deadly jellyfish.
4 He is planning to write a book about his experiences, and he might accept a new contract with Tourism Queensland.

## 2

2, 4, 5 and 9

## 3

1 a beachside mansion
2 a busy schedule
3 press conferences
4 administrative duties
5 tweeted
6 get the chance
7 rushed
8 immensely

## 4

1 a brilliant    b boiling
2 a terrible    b furious
3 a tiny    b delicious
4 a impossible    b exhausted
5 a fascinating    b huge

## 5

1 to  2 used  3 would  4 used  5 used
6 would  7 use  8 used

## 6A

1 Did you use to spend your holidays by the sea?
2 We didn't use to have a dog when I was a child.
3 Daniel used to be one of the naughtiest boys in the class, but he's much better now.
4 I used to love reading in the evening, but now I'm too tired.
5 I remember how I used to sit in my grandfather's studio and watch him paint.
6 I used to be quite fat. Then, I went on a diet and lost ten kilos.
7 Children always used to play around on the streets in the old days, but there's nobody here now.
8 They used to live in a big house but they had to move.

**B**

Sentences 1, 5, 7

**7B**

1 /s/  2 /z/  3 /s/  4 /s/  5 /z/
6 /z/  7 /s/  8 /s/

**8A**

1 Dear Ms Nelson
2 I am writing to you about …
3 I am currently studying English …
4 I believe that my communication skills …
5 Thank you for your consideration. If you require …
6 Yours sincerely
7 Vinnie Jessop

**B**

1 at your earliest convenience
2 I believe I meet all the requirements of the post
3 proven ability at
4 hands-on
5 regarding
6 I would like to submit an application

## 4.3

**1A**

1 b  2 a  3 c  4 a  5 b  6 c  7 b  8 c

**B**

1 difficult boss
2 successful businessman
3 work, team
4 go, interview
5 earn, six-figure
6 get fired

**2**

1 see things
2 that's a good idea
3 suggest we think about
4 That's fine
5 not sure that I agree
6 see what you mean
7 How about if we

**3**

1 on  2 all  3 on  4 recap  5 to  6 up

## REVIEW AND CHECK 2

**1**

1 a  2 c  3 b  4 b  5 a  6 a  7 b  8 c

**2**

1 a chat          b apologise
2 a moaning       b warn
3 a argue         b gossip
4 a complimented  b boast
5 a shortly       b near
6 a year          b term
7 a long          b short
8 a years'        b Next

**3**

1 aren't likely to
2 might not
3 may
4 is going to
5 is likely to
6 will
7 won't
8 may
9 are going to
10 could

**4**

1 a piece of cake
2 in hot water
3 my foot in it
4 close to my heart
5 the rat race
6 give me a hand
7 on my mind
8 my cup of tea
9 keep an eye on
10 run out of time

**5**

1 catch  2 lost  3 get  4 exactly  5 mean
6 say  7 repeat  8 saying  9 what  10 other

**6**

1 competitive
2 leader
3 amazing
4 exhausted
5 risk taker
6 freezing
7 fascinating
8 salary
9 boss, fired
10 interview
11 furious
12 hard-working

**7B**

oOo: successful, delicious, exhausted
Ooo: interview, furious, difficult
Oo: tasty, leader, boiling, freezing
oOoo: competitive, impossible

**8**

1 has to
2 should
3 mustn't
4 don't have to
5 must / have to
6 mustn't
7 must / have to
8 have to
9 shouldn't
10 don't have to

**9**

1 remember  2 forgotten  3 left  4 listen
5 hear  6 won  7 funny  8 fun

**10A**

1 used to live
2 used to work
3 used to study
4 used to have
5 would play
6 would enjoy

**B**

1 didn't use to have
2 didn't use to work
3 used to enjoy
4 didn't use to wear
5 didn't use to stay
6 would eat

**11A**

1 that  2 me  3 agree  4 should
5 things  6 don't  7 point  8 about
9 sure  10 suggest  11 What  12 need

**B**

**opinions:** I feel that, I think we should think about, The way I see things, Why don't we, How about if we, I suggest we focus on, How about, I think we need to focus on

**responses:** That's OK by me, I'm not sure that I agree, That's a good idea, I'm not sure that's a good idea

### TEST

1 b  2 b  3 a  4 c  5 b  6 c  7 b  8 a  9 b
10 c  11 b  12 a  13 c  14 c  15 a  16 b
17 c  18 b  19 a  20 c  21 c  22 b  23 a
24 c  25 a  26 c  27 a  28 b  29 c  30 a

# UNIT 5

## 5.1

### 1A
1 vaccinations
2 electricity
3 nuclear power
4 computer network
5 antibiotics
6 space travel
7 motorbikes

### B
1 genetic engineering
2 nuclear power
3 antibiotics
4 electricity
5 space travel
6 communications satellites
7 solar power
8 vaccination

### 2B
/eɪ/ **make:** sp**a**ce, communic**a**tions, **a**eroplanes, vaccin**a**tions

/æ/ **apple:** **a**ntibiotics, tr**a**vel, s**a**tellites, v**a**cuum

/ə/ **polar:** nucle**a**r, m**a**chine, commerci**a**l, sol**a**r

### 3A
1 T  2 O  3 M

### B
1 a  2 c  3 b  4 c  5 a  6 b

### 4
1 more expensive than
2 better
3 easier
4 bigger
5 heavier
6 the lightest
7 smaller
8 cheaper

### 5
1 much
2 a little bit
3 by far
4 a lot
5 a bit
6 slightly

### 6A
1 ✔  2 ✗  3 ✔  4 ✗  5 ✗  6 ✔

### B
Plan B is better because it is more clearly organised into advantages and disadvantages. The paragraphs are planned and there is an introduction and a conclusion.

### C
**However,** there are also disadvantages.

**One of the main advantages is that** when you study online, you …

**The problem is that** when you study online, there is … students. **Another disadvantage is** you might find it difficult … your studies. **And another thing,** you might experience …

**In my opinion,** online courses offer students more choice and flexibility. **However,** they are …

## 5.2

### 1
**Not possible:**
2 wonder
3 enquire
4 questioned
5 wonder
6 responded
7 look into
8 enquires

### 2
2 question
3 look into
4 debate
5 response
6 investigating
7 enquired
8 reply
9 wondered

### 3
1 aren't you
2 didn't she
3 have they
4 will he
5 doesn't it
6 did we
7 has it
8 won't you
9 does it
10 didn't you

### 4
2 was funny, wasn't it
3 won't crash the car, will he
4 wasn't a very good game, was it
5 write to me, won't you
6 didn't miss the last bus, did you
7 speak French, don't you
8 haven't seen my watch, have you

### 5A
1, 3, and 5 are genuine questions.

### 6C
1 Which food
2 about stress
3 good for you
4 eat rotting food
5 amount of water turn into ice

### D
2 dose  3 smog  4 rotting  5 hatch

### 7
1 responsible  2 hopeless  3 creative
4 easy  5 effective  6 successful  7 valuable
8 profitable

## 5.3

### 1
1 down  2 recharging  3 order  4 fixing
5 switching  6 crashed  7 work  8 sort
9 memory  10 print

### 2A
A 3  He wants to know if they have to bring anything.

B 4  She wants someone to hold something for her.

C 7  She wants someone to pick her up at the station.

D 2  He wants to know what time the bank opens.

E 1  She wants to know the way to the swimming pool.

F 8  She wants to know if there is a post office near there.

G 6  He wants to know what time the (afternoon) show starts.

H 5  She wants someone to open the door for her.

### B
1 could, course
2 know, sure
3 you, of
4 help, sorry
5 opening, not
6 tell, Let
7 mind, Sure
8 if, there

### 3
1 No, of course not.
2 I'm not sure. Let me have a look.
3 Yes, of course.
4 I'm afraid I can't.
5 Yes I can.

## UNIT 6

### 6.1

#### 1A

1 exhausting  2 worried  3 boring
4 annoyed  5 frightening  6 embarrassed
7 confused  8 relaxing  9 satisfied
10 shocked

#### B

1 boring  2 annoyed  3 exhausting
4 satisfied  5 confusing  6 embarrassed
7 shocking  8 relaxing

#### 2B

**Reasons:** You're irritated with someone,
You're frustrated about something,
People criticise you.

**Consequences:** You start to shout, You
throw things around, You feel tense.

**Solutions:** You do physical exercise, You
try meditation, You distance yourself
from the situation.

#### 3

1 increases
2 understand
3 solve
4 situations / things
5 change
6 distance
7 breathing / breaths
8 calmly

#### 4A

1 finds, will / 'll leave
2 will get, works
3 exercise, live
4 leave, will / 'll miss
5 will / 'll start, is
6 is, dance
7 is, eat
8 use, won't get

#### B

2 specific – first conditional
3 general – zero conditional
4 specific – first conditional
5 specific – first conditional
6 general– zero conditional
7 general– zero conditional
8 specific – first conditional

#### 5

2 If **you go** to England, …
3 I'll tell him you called when **I see** him.
4 ✔
5 If they arrive early, **will you ask** them
to wait?
6 If **you come** to the party tonight, will
you bring a friend?
7 When I go to Krakow, **I usually see** my
aunt.
8 ✔
9 She will get angry if **you say** that!
10 **I'll / will go** to the doctor tomorrow if
I feel worse.

#### 6A

1 c  2 c  3 a  4 c  5 c  6 b  7 a  8 b

#### B

1 down  2 on  3 up  4 off  5 on  6 up
7 off  8 off

### 6.2

#### 1

1 do, experiments
2 watch, programme
3 get, seat
4 hold, sale
5 jump, queue
6 cut, hair
7 raise money

#### 2

2 If she was fast enough, she would /
could play for the team.
3 We could drive to your house if we
had a car.
4 They would pass the exam if they
studied.
5 My life wouldn't be so easy if I didn't
have a supportive family.
6 If I had the money, I would buy that
house.
7 I would write to my friends if I wasn't
so lazy.
8 If you watered your plants regularly,
they wouldn't look so dry!
9 They would help in the house if their
mother asked them.
10 If I didn't work on Saturdays, I could
come to the barbecue.

#### 3

2 had
3 would be
4 would introduce
5 had to
6 would change
7 was
8 would be
9 would make
10 wouldn't let
11 was
12 wouldn't have

#### 4A

1 If I had more time, I'd learn to ski.
2 If you didn't work, what would you
do?
3 If they had to move, they wouldn't
live with me.
4 She'd go out at night if her parents let
her.
5 Where would you go if you had the
chance?
6 I wouldn't sleep if I drank that coffee.

#### 5A

The topic is which kinds of people are
likely to be victims of crime.

#### B

2, 3, 4, 6 and 7 are potential victims.

#### D

2 Yes, (because she isn't) paying
attention to what's happening around
her. She isn't looking at other people.
3 Yes, (because they are concentrating
on the map, not) the people around
them.
4 Yes, (because he didn't put the
money) in his wallet quickly.
5 No, (because of her positive) body
language. She's confident, she knows
where she's going, she's looking
straight ahead, and she's probably
moving fast.
6 Yes, (because he's looking at his feet
and he doesn't know) who's around
him.
7 Yes, (because rule number one of
the street is: if you have anything
valuable,) don't show it.

#### 6A

Summary c

#### B

1 D  2 C  3 B  4 A

#### C

Maybe, It's possible that, probably, in all
likelihood, In all probability

## 6.3

### 1A
1 pass  2 accident  3 offered  4 place
5 engaged  6 lost  7 failed  8 split  9 won
10 promoted  11 degree  12 bought

### B
2 e  3 d  4 a  5 b  6 c

### 2A
A 4  B 3  C 1  D 8  E 2  F 7  G 6  H 5

### B
1 Bad news, ~~as~~ I'm afraid.
2 I'm sorry ~~for~~ to have to tell you, but we lost the match.
3 I've got some good ~~unfortunately~~ news for you.
4 I'm afraid ~~of~~ I've got some bad news.
5 There's something ~~who~~ I've got to tell you.
6 You'll never guess what ~~is~~ happened.
7 ~~It's~~ unfortunately, we were burgled last night.
8 I've got something ~~for~~ to tell you.

### 3
1 Congratulations, fantastic
2 terrible, sorry
3 Well done, great news
4 awful
5 Have, lucky
6 shame
7 joking

## REVIEW AND CHECK 3

### 1
1 electricity
2 vaccination
3 space travel
4 genetic engineering
5 solar panels
6 computer network
7 nuclear power
8 commercial aeroplanes

### 2
1 is slightly warmer
2 are far more expensive than
3 the most delicious meal
4 was a lot easier than
5 the simplest
6 much happier
7 a bit shorter than
8 a worse place than

### 3
1 discuss  2 respond  3 look
4 wondering  5 research  6 investigate
7 inquiries  8 debate

### 4
1 can't we       5 wasn't it
2 haven't they   6 didn't you
3 won't we       7 will you
4 do you         8 have you

### 5
1 painful  2 homeless  3 responsible
4 creative  5 hopeless  6 effective
7 thankful  8 messy

### 6
1 The car's broken down.
2 My phone needs recharging.
3 It's out of order.
4 The printer needs fixing.
5 Try switching it off and on again.
6 It keeps making this strange noise.
7 It doesn't work any more.
8 We have to sort it out.

### 7
1 tell, of course
2 if there's, sure
3 checking, course
4 see, look

### 8
1 annoyed  2 relaxed  3 confusing
4 bored  5 embarrassing  6 exhausted
7 worried  8 frightening

### 9A
1 I'll call  2 don't  3 is  4 will die  5 I'd
6 didn't  7 would  8 don't  9 live
10 get  11 would  12 had

### B
1 b  2 c  3 a  4 a  5 c  6 b  7 a  8 c

### 10
1 up  2 down  3 on  4 on  5 off  6 on
7 off  8 down  9 off  10 down

### 11
1 b  2 b  3 b  4 c  5 a  6 c  7 b

### 12
1 c  2 e  3 a  4 g  5 h  6 b  7 f  8 d

### 3
1 A: I'm sorry to have to **tell** you, but the train has been cancelled.
   B: **That's** annoying.
2 A: I've got **some** good news for you.
   B: **Congratulations!**
3 A: There's something I've got to **tell you**.
   B: Oh. I'm sorry **to** hear that.
4 A: You'll never **guess what**.
   B: **That's fantastic** news!
5 A: **Unfortunately,** I didn't get the job.
   B: That's **a** real shame.

### TEST
1 c  2 b  3 a  4 b  5 c  6 c  7 b  8 c  9 b
10 a  11 c  12 a  13 c  14 b  15 b  16 c
17 a  18 c  19 a  20 b  21 c  22 b  23 c
24 a  25 b  26 a  27 c  28 b  29 b  30 c

## UNIT 7

### 7.1

### 1
2 focus on
3 hard at
4 get better
5 high achiever
6 believe in

### 3
1 DK  2 T  3 F  4 T  5 F  6 F

### 4
1 e  2 b  3 c  4 a  5 f  6 d

### 5
1 've / have been going
2 've / have been waiting
3 haven't been sleeping
4 's / has been crying
5 've / have known
6 've / have been skiing
7 have … been living
8 Have … been watching, have … enjoyed / been enjoying

### 6
1 has been happening
2 haven't had
3 have been staying
4 has been working
5 've / have been thinking
6 haven't decided
7 've / have been looking
8 have found
9 've / have been working
10 's / has been studying

### 7A
1 depend on
2 succeed in
3 pay attention to
4 rely on
5 pick up on
6 have a talent for
7 think about
8 have access to

**B**

1 think about

2 pay attention to

3 depends on

4 pick up on

5 have a talent for

6 have access to

7 succeed in

8 rely on

## 7.2

### 1A

1 c 2 a 3 b 4 c 5 a 6 b 7 a 8 c

### B

1 hopeless, useless

2 gifted, talented

3 skilful

4 expert

5 have a lot of ability, have an aptitude for

### 2

1 couldn't 2 manage 3 remember 4 was 5 could 6 to 7 wasn't 8 managed

### 3

**Not possible:**

1 didn't manage

2 do able to

3 could

4 can

5 are manage to

6 didn't able to

7 'm not manage to

8 could to

9 Do you can

10 Could you

### 4A

1 ✔

2 a 6 syllables, b 5 syllables

3 ✔

4 a 6 syllables, b 7 syllables

### 5B

A When Sidis was seven months, he pointed at the moon and said 'moon'.

B At eighteen months, he could read *The New York Times*.

C At six, he could speak Russian, French, German and Hebrew.

D Aged nine, he gave a lecture on mathematics at Harvard University.

E Journalists followed him around and wrote articles about him but he didn't achieve much as an adult.

F He died in 1944, aged 46.

## C

1 His parents were from Russia. They moved to New York.

2 William's first word was 'door'.

3 William was six when he could speak Russian, French, German and Hebrew.

4 When he was nine, he gave a lecture on mathematics at Harvard University.

5 Two years later, he began attending Harvard University.

6 Journalists 'followed him around'.

7 His sister said he knew all the languages of the world and that he could learn a language in a day.

8 For most of his adult life, Sidis was 'running away' from fame.

### 6A

1 **Mistakes:** His first word was *door*, not *moon*

He took one day to learn a language, not one week.

2 **Exact words:** Journalists followed him around and wrote articles about this young genius

Not all childhood geniuses will produce great things as adults

### B

1 Uni (university), yrs (years)

2 &

3 close 2 him

4 THE LIFE OF WILLIAM SIDIS

5 Background

6 leave people alone

## 7.3

### 1

1 an MA

2 face-to-face learning

3 an apprenticeship

4 qualifications

5 a certificate

6 a degree

7 a PhD

8 an online course

9 distance learning

10 a driving licence

### 2A

1 b 2 c 3 c

### B

1 a 2 b 3 b 4 b 5 a 6 b 7 b 8 a 9 a 10 b

## UNIT 8

### 8.1

### 1

2 Can I **ask a** favour?

3 Whenever they're arguing, I prefer to mind **my own** business.

4 Hayley has invited **us over** for dinner at her house.

5 Those neighbours are **a nuisance** – they're always …

6 She got **to know** her neighbours immediately.

7 Please don't **disturb me**.

8 One thing that gets **on my** nerves is when …

9 Xun hasn't made **friends with** her neighbours yet …

10 I keep myself **to myself**.

### 2

2 Have you received **the** letter I sent you?

3 ✔

4 Do you have **a** pen I can borrow?

5 ✔

6 Is there **an** airport in the city?

7 I'm going to Germany in **the** morning.

8 We live by **the** Pacific Ocean.

9 My brother is **an** actor.

10 ✔

11 ✔

12 Did you see **the** film I told you about?

13 I live in **the** United States.

14 She's **the** nicest woman I know.

15 ✔

### 3

2 b vi There are plenty of good restaurants in the town, especially if you like French food.

3 f iii I don't know much about this city, but I like the architecture.

4 a v All of us love this place because it's so friendly.

5 g vii If you have enough time, go to the museum – it's great.

6 c viii There are too many cars in most big cities – I hate traffic!

7 e i I've got lots of friends in this community.

8 h ii I spent a bit of time in Poland when I was younger.

### 4

3 but 4 of 5 ✔ 6 ✔ 7 ✔ 8 to (money) 9 small 10 ✔ 11 a (five hours) 12 more 13 ✔ 14 all 15 ✔ 16 ✔ 17 a

## 5A

1 Elise's neighbours are her parents and her brother's family. Marc's neighbours are 'a couple of cows' / a farmer.

2 Elise likes this situation because they 'help each other'. Marc likes the situation because they 'just love the peace and quiet'.

3 Elise sees her neighbours every day. They work together and they all eat together once or twice a week. Marc never sees his neighbours, apart from the cows.

4 Elise has lived there all her life. Marc has lived there for ten years.

### B

1 perfect  2 family  3 eleven  4 Sunday
5 normal  6 husband  7 ten  8 Paris
9 transport  10 farmhouse  11 online
12 first

### C

1 a  2 b  3 b  4 b  5 b  6 a

## 6A

2 high street
3 housing estate
4 sports centre
5 industrial estate
6 car park
7 supermarket
8 language school
9 shopping centre
10 one-way street
11 terraced houses
12 outdoor market
13 gift shop
14 primary school

## 7

1 housing estate
2 language school
3 primary school
4 one-way street
5 sports centre
6 terraced houses
7 traffic lights
8 car park
9 supermarket
10 gift shop
11 outdoor market
12 industrial estate
13 high street
14 shopping centre

## 8.2

### 1

2 j  3 f  4 k  5 b  6 l  7 i  8 e  9 h  10 c
11 d  12 g

### 2

3 a  4 b  5 b  6 a  7 b  8 a

### 3

1 clothing that      5 which has
2 place where        6 thing that
3 person who         7 who behaves
4 name that          8 a place

### 4

1 a  2 a  3 b  4 a  5 b

## 5A

A CouchSurfer is a traveller who arranges to stay on a stranger's couch.

### B

1 He had nowhere to sleep.

2 He wrote to 1,500 students in Reykjavik, and he had dozens of replies inviting him to stay.

3 The website says CouchSurfing focuses on cross-cultural sharing.

4 1 You type the name of the city. 2 You look at the profiles of people there and choose someone.  3 You contact them to see if they are free. 4 They may ask you to meet for a coffee first before inviting you to their home.

5 You can read what other CouchSurfers say about this person, and there is also a system of 'vouching', in which other people promise that your host has a good character.

### C

1 e  2 c  3 b  4 a  5 d

## 6A

1 feature  2 like  3 would  4 best

### B

1 B  2 A  3 D  4 C

## 8.3

### 1

1 Help yourself
2 Excuse the mess
3 Make yourself at home
4 Be my guest
5 Have a seat
6 Put your feet up

### C

A 2  B 5  C 1  D 3  E 4  F 6

### 2

1 a  2 b  3 a  4 b  5 b  6 b  7 a  8 b  9 b
10 a

### 3

1 It's no problem.
2 Not at all.
3 That's all right.
4 It's fine.
5 It's nothing.
6 You really don't have to.
7 We can sort it out.

## REVIEW AND CHECK 4

### 1

1 Our company focuses **on** quality software.

2 ✔

3 It's important that we work **hard** at this.

4 The key is to believe **in** yourself.

5 ✔

6 We'll improve if **we practise** every day.

### 2

1 known
2 been waiting
3 been reading
4 invited
5 been working
6 been learning
7 seen
8 met

### 3

1 to  2 to  3 on  4 in  5 for  6 on  7 on
8 about  9 with  10 at / for  11 to
12 to  13 in  14 for  15 in  16 with
17 about  18 for

### 4

1 Because he's an expert in his subject.

2 Because he has a lot of ability in maths.

3 Because she's gifted at the sport.

4 Because they have a talent for writing scripts.

5 Because he has an aptitude for the game.

6 Because I'm absolutely hopeless at science.

### 5

1 We can't play
2 She can sing
3 Are you able
4 didn't manage to
5 wasn't able to
6 manage to clean
7 could you speak
8 managed to break

### 6

1 qualifications  2 licence
3 apprenticeship  4 learning  5 distance
6 online  7 degree  8 Master's

### 7A

1 view  2 reason  3 For  4 must  5 For
6 another  7 For  8 what  9 said  10 do
11 give  12 said

### B

O: 1, 2, 3, 4, 10

E: 5, 6, 7, 11

R: 8, 9, 12

## 8

2 myself to myself
3 doing me favours
4 your own business
5 over for dinner
6 get on well

## 9

2 ✔, ✔
3 ✔, **the** best ones
4 ✔, **the** rat
5 **the** party, too **many** people
6 ✔, **a** haircut
7 ✔, **the** Moon
8 too **much** time, ✔
9 ✔, **a** lot of pepper
10 ✔, **Barcelona**

## 10

2 house 3 calling 4 school
5 apartment 6 news 7 shops 8 flat

## 11

2 ✔
3 Corporate websites
4 Ratings sites
5 ✔
6 Personal homepages
7 ✔
8 ✔
9 ✔
10 dating sites
11 ✔
12 Blogs

## 12

1 who I spoke to was very nice
2 which / that we visited had a wonderful exhibition
3 where she was born is now under water
4 who is in the fashion industry, lives in Paris
5 where I grew up is now a theatre
6 who is my best friend, works with my father
7 which lasted for ten days, is now finished
8 which they went to / where they went served crocodile

## 13

1 have 2 Be 3 Excuse 4 Make 5 put 6 help

## 14

1
Pete: Do I need ~~for~~ to bring anything?
Don: No, it's not ~~the~~ necessary.

2
Kat: It's considered ~~be~~ a bit rude.
Kat: It's OK – we can sort it ~~but~~ out.

3
Andre: Is this ~~for~~ a bad time?
Bella: Can you ~~to~~ come back in ten minutes?
Andre: I didn't ~~can~~ realise you were in a meeting.
Bella: Don't ~~to~~ worry about it.

4
Nick: What should we ~~to~~ do?
Tam: No, you'd better ~~be~~ not.

## 15

2 B: It's **no** problem. I can photocopy mine.
3 B: That's **all right**. It didn't hurt.
4 B: Not **at** all. We usually don't start till 3.15.
5 B: No, **it's** nothing. I didn't even feel it.
6 B: Honestly, **it's** fine. Don't worry about it.

### TEST

1 b 2 c 3 b 4 a 5 c 6 c 7 c 8 c 9 c
10 a 11 c 12 a 13 b 14 a 15 c 16 b
17 c 18 a 19 a 20 b 21 a 22 b 23 c
24 a 25 c 26 a 27 a 28 c 29 c 30 a

### UNIT 9

### 9.1

### 1A

1 revolution
2 turning point
3 development
4 spread
5 advance
6 movement
7 invention
8 foundation
9 discovery
10 progress

### B

1 discovery
2 spread
3 development
4 progress
5 advances
6 movement
7 revolution
8 invention

### 2

1 c 2 c 3 b 4 a 5 b 6 c 7 a 8 a

### 3

2 If Archduke Ferdinand hadn't been assassinated, World War I wouldn't have started.
3 If people from Sumer hadn't needed permanent records, they wouldn't have invented writing.
4 If World War II hadn't happened, the United Nations wouldn't have (been) formed in 1945.
5 If William the Conqueror hadn't invaded England in 1066, the English language wouldn't have changed.
6 If Charles Darwin hadn't travelled to South America, he wouldn't have developed the theory of evolution.
7 If sailors on the *Titanic* had seen the iceberg, 1,595 people wouldn't have died.
8 If Captain James Cook hadn't sailed to Australia, it wouldn't have become a British colony.

### 4A

1 If I'**d** known you were coming, I **would've** waited.
2 If I'**d** waited, I **would've** been late.
3 If I'**d been** late, I **would've** missed the show.
4 If I'**d** missed the show I **would've** wasted my money.
5 If I'**d** wasted my money, I **would've** been angry.

### 5A

2 Ancient Greece, over 3,000
3 China, over 2,000
4 Ancient Greece / Korea, over 2,000
5 Egypt / Persia (Iran), more than 2,000

### B

A Ancient Greek toothpaste used oyster shells.
B Hannibal used snakes as a biological weapon.
C The Inuit played a type of football.
D A rich English banker installed central heating in his house so he could grow grapes.
E In ancient sculptures from Egypt and Persia, only kings or very important people had umbrellas.

## C

a enemy  b symbol  c installed
d infected  e crushed

## 6A

b  The History of Writing

## B

1  In 3200 BC, Sumerians invented writing.
2  While
3  As a result

# 9.2

## 1A/B

I grew up in a big old house with a big old family. The house had four floors, one floor for each generation. The bottom floor was where my maternal grandparents lived. **They were given** the bottom floor so that they didn't have to climb any steps – that's the story I <u>was told</u> anyway. But in reality, I think it's because my grandmother escaped the house at 4a.m. every morning to go for walks and we didn't want **to be woken up**. Mum and Dad's room was on the second floor, and us children **were put** on the third floor, out of the way. At the very top of the steps there was an attic where my great-grandfather <u>was hidden</u> away, out of sight. He was as mad as a box of frogs. He used to play operas on an ancient gramophone and sing Puccini at the top of his voice. When he died, I <u>was given</u> that gramophone and all his records. Amazingly, forty years later, it still works. The house **has been rebuilt** many times since those days and the garden, where we used to climb trees and run wild, <u>has been covered</u> with concrete. I read recently that the house **will be sold** again. It <u>won't be bought</u> by me, though. My memories are enough.

## 2A

2  One day a cure for cancer will be discovered.
3  The files were stolen last year.
4  These famous photos were taken at the end of the war.
5  The President hasn't been told about the plan.
6  The missing people have been found.
7  All flights going out of Paris were cancelled.
8  The paintings are cleaned once a year.

## B

The auxiliary verbs *are*, *were*, *has(n't)
been* and *have been* are contracted (said in a shortened version).

## 3

2  over a quarter-century
3  just over a century ago
4  millennium
5  over seven decades
6  the generation
7  just over a fortnight
8  half a century

## 4A

1  have a good time
2  make progress
3  give a talk
4  come naturally
5  have a break
6  have a dream
7  come first
8  give instructions
9  give directions
10  have trouble
11  come back
12  make a mess
13  give me a call
14  make a profit
15  come by car
16  make a decision

## B

1  having trouble, have a break
2  made a decision, made a profit
3  give me a call, give me directions
4  come naturally, came first
5  give a talk, give instructions

## 5A

1  around 1880–1895
2  1945 to about 1960
3  A novel: *Generation X: Tales for an Accelerated Culture*
4  Rebelling against their parents' values, not wanting to work for the same company their whole life, listening to 'grunge' music, playing video games
5  between 1980s and 1990s
6  Love of technology, amazing networkers, constantly online, great multi-taskers

## B

1  Socrates say (about the younger generation)
2  begin naming each generation
3  people were killed in World War I
4  after the Second World War (from 1945–1960)
5  wrote *Millennials Rising: The Next Great Generation* / first described Generation Y in detail
6  people used the internet in 2010

## C

1 e  2 d  3 c  4 a  5 b  6 f

# 9.3

## 1

1 brave  2 charismatic  3 exemplary
4 influential  5 inspirational  6 creative
7 original  8 innovative

## 2

1 a  2 b  3 b  4 a  5 b  6 a  7 b  8 a

## 3A

1 Did  2 That  3 Was  4 Doesn't  5 say
6 Do  7 remember  8 Haven't  9 didn't
10 Will

# UNIT 10

# 10.1

## 1A

1  on standby
2  double glazed
3  processed
4  insulated
5  organic
6  pre-prepared
7  packaging
8  energy-saving
9  recycled
10  second-hand

## B

1  organic
2  second-hand
3  double glazed
4  energy-saving
5  pre-prepared
6  processed
7  recycled
8  standby
9  packaging
10  insulated

## 2A

1 lights  2 Eiffel Tower  3 Pyramids
4 Sydney  5 change  6 different

## 3A

1 F (2.2 million people)
2 T
3 T
4 F (Some people think the event is meaningless.)
5 T
6 F (He doesn't think the event helps people to change their behaviour.)

## B

1 stand 2 global 3 part 4 plunged
5 attention 6 raise 7 waste

## 4

1 didn't 2 were 3 had 4 her 5 next
6 his 7 would 8 they

## 5A

A: I want to go to Spain, because I've never been there before.
T: How are you planning to travel?
A: I'm thinking of going by plane.
T: Have you thought about taking the train instead?
A: No, I haven't, but it's a good idea.
T: It's cheaper than flying. I'll show you some of the train routes.
A: OK.
T: Have you decided where you want to stay?
A: No, I haven't. Could you show me what accommodation is available?
T: There's an eco-farm near Valencia where you can stay for free, if you help the farmer pick his olives.
A: That sounds great!

## B

2 asked her, was planning
3 she was thinking
4 she'd thought
5 she hadn't, it was
6 would show her
7 had decided, she wanted
8 she hadn't
9 could stay, helped
10 sounded great

## 6

1 misunderstood
2 disobey
3 reuse
4 unusual
5 underestimated
6 disappeared
7 untidy
8 renew
9 unethical
10 disagree

## 10.2

### 1

1 c 2 b 3 a 4 c 5 a 6 b 7 c

### 2A

A 4 B 5 C 2 D 1 E 3

### 3

1 Jorge 2 Irene 3 Claire 4 Claire
5 Mariella 6 Irene

### 4

1 pleasant
2 water
3 yellow middle
4 soft; liquid
5 pasta
6 sad because you haven't got

### 5

2 suggested spending
3 invited us to stay
4 offered to take
5 explained that it would be / explained that it was
6 recommended that we travel / recommended travelling
7 agreed to choose
8 warned us not to go
9 promise to write

### 6A

1 refused to come
2 promised to call
3 decided to go
4 agreed not to go
5 warned us that
6 invited James to go
7 explained that the children
8 recommended buying

### B

unstressed

### 7A

The writer doesn't recommend the restaurant because they thought the atmosphere was uninviting, the service was poor and the food was not great, either.

### B

a so 2
b Although 4
c unless 5
d such, that 3
e While 1

### 8A

1 no information given
2 no information given
3 ✔
4 ✔
5 ✔

## 10.3

### 1

1 passport
2 check in
3 aisle
4 boarding card
5 X-ray machine
6 board
7 priority boarding
8 proceed to gate number
9 hand luggage

### 2

1 b 2 c 3 a 4 b 5 c 6 a 7 b 8 a

### 3

1 c 2 a 3 f 4 d 5 e 6 b

## REVIEW AND CHECK 5

### 1

1 revolution 2 turning point
3 development 4 spread 5 advance
6 movement 7 invention
8 foundation 9 discovery 10 progress

### 2

1 hadn't helped, wouldn't have finished
2 would have gone, hadn't rained
3 'd / had studied, wouldn't have failed
4 would have told, 'd / had had
5 hadn't scored, wouldn't have won
6 would you have done, 'd / had missed

### 3

1 are sold here
2 isn't produced in England
3 is being built
4 was assassinated
5 wasn't written by Samuel Beckett
6 haven't been told anything about the exam

### 4

1 millennium
2 a decade
3 a fortnight
4 a quarter-century
5 generation
6 the nineties

### 5

**Not possible:**
1 well
2 a discussion
3 project
4 homework
5 forward
6 problem
7 money
8 progress

**6**

1 creative  2 original  3 charismatic
4 exemplary  5 innovative  6 brave
7 inspirational  8 influential

**7**

2  c  i  I haven't a clue.

3  a  iii  I'm fairly sure it's Jane.

4  f  iv  It's definitely not Sarah.

5  d  ii  I'm sure it isn't Elizabeth.

6  e  vi  I have no idea.

**8**

1 just about  2 Is  3 interesting
4 couldn't

**9**

1  organic

2  energy-saving, insulated

3  double glazed, on standby

4  pre-prepared, packaging

5  second-hand, recycled

**10**

2  you didn't know the answer

3  you had been to Germany

4  you could swim

5  you weren't going to university

6  you would be there on Monday

7  you wouldn't be able to help

8  you hadn't spoken to Kevin

**11**

1  He asked me **when the game started**.

2  He asked me if **I play / played any instruments**.

3  ✔

4  ✔

5  He asked me why **I was crying**.

6  She asked me if **my baby slept all night**.

7  She asked me if **they spoke** English.

**12**

1  misunderstood, unusual

2  misjudged, overcooked

3  unbelievable, overweight

4  untidy, disobeyed

5  reuse, recycle

6  disapproved, unethical

7  underestimate, renew

8  disappeared, unknown

**13**

1  David promised (invited) us to his birthday party. Sentence 6

2  The tour guide refused (warned) us about poisonous spiders. Sentence 3

3  The doorman suggested (refused) to let me into the club because I was wearing jeans. Sentence 7

4  I explained (offered) to take my host family for dinner, to say 'thank you'. Sentence 5

5  The teacher invited (explained) the grammar clearly so everyone understood. Sentence 1

6  My dad warned (promised) to buy me an ice cream if I behaved well. Sentence 2

7  Minty offered (suggested) going to Greece for our holiday. Sentence 4

**14**

1  that I

2  that

3  me to

4  me

5  to wait

6  to take

7  to give

8  to move

9  to

10  trying

**15**

1 d  2 a  3 e  4 g  5 b  6 h  7 c  8 f

**16**

1  the most important thing is to

2  make sure you bring

3  watch out for snakes

4  it's not very common

5  if I were you, I'd start

6  you need to bring

7  have a tendency to bring

8  Whatever you do, don't pack

9  don't forget to bring

10  on the whole

11  be careful to eat

12  you'd better take some

TEST

1 a  2 c  3 b  4 c  5 c  6 b  7 a  8 a  9 c
10 c  11 b  12 b  13 c  14 b  15 c  16 a
17 a  18 c  19 b  20 c  21 c  22 a  23 b
24 c  25 a  26 b  27 b  28 a  29 b  30 b

**Pearson Education Ltd**
Edinburgh Gate
Harlow
Essex CM20 2JE
England
and Associated Companies throughout the world.

www.pearsonelt.com

© Pearson Education Limited 2011

The rights of Antonia Clare and JJ Wilson to be identified as the authors of this Work has been asserted by them in accordance with the Copyright, Designs and Patents Act 1988.

All rights reserved; no part of this publication may be reproduced, stored in a retrieval system, or transmitted in any form or by any means, electronic, mechanical, photocopying, recording, or otherwise without the prior written permission of the Publishers.

First published 2011

Third impression 2012

ISBN 978-1-4082-5949-8

Set in Gill Sans 9.75/11.5

Printed in Slovakia by Neografia

Illustrations by 195 Eric (kja-artists.com): pp9, 13, 24, 27, 38, 54; 087 Sean (kja-artists.com): pp8, 11, 18, 22, 36, 40, 41, 46, 49, 55, 61, 67, 68

**Acknowledgements**

Text
We are grateful to the following for permission to reproduce copyright material:
Extract on page 54 adapted from 'CouchSurfers - The Community that won't lie down', www.couchsurfing.org <outbind://35/www.couchsurfing.org> , ³CouchSurfing² and ³CouchSurfer² are registered and unregistered service marks of CouchSurfing International, Inc. - a Non-Profit Organization www.couchsurfing.org <outbind://35/www.couchsurfing.org>
In some instances we have been unable to trace the owners of copyright material, and we would appreciate any information that would enable us to do so.

Photo
The publisher would like to thank the following for their kind permission to reproduce their photographs:
(Key: b-bottom; c-centre; l-left; r-right; t-top)
Alamy Images: Cultura 4, Danita Delimont 24tr, David Gee 4 13, Image Source 7, moodboard 24cl, Radius Images 24cr; Corbis: Bettmann 20, 34; Earth Hour: 65; Getty Images: Graham Chadwick / ALLSPORT 64l, Rick Graves 23, TORSTEN BLACKWOOD / AFP 25b; Kobal Collection Ltd: 48r, WARNER BROS. 10; Pearson Education Ltd: Studio 8 39br; Press Association Images: ABACA Press France 64r, Brian Cassey, File 25t; Reuters: Casper Christoffersen / Scanpix 64c; Rex Features: DAVID HARTLEY 48tl, SHAROK HATAMI 48c; Thinkstock: Ableimages 39bl, Comstock Images 24tl, Digital Vision 50, Hemera 24br, 69c, iStockphoto 51, 66, 69t, Jack Hollingsworth / Stockbyte 24bl, Jupiterimages 27, 39tr, 69b, Nick Daly 39tl

All other images © Pearson Education

Every effort has been made to trace the copyright holders and we apologise in advance for any unintentional omissions. We would be pleased to insert the appropriate acknowledgement in any subsequent edition of this publication.

Picture Research by: Kay Altwegg